This edition of *Vegetarian Kitchen* was printed in July 2016 by Thermomix in Australia Pty Ltd.

National Library of Australia
Cataloguing-in-Publication entry
Title: Vegetarian Kitchen
ISBN: 978-0-9924673-8-8

Thermomix in Australia Pty Ltd
Phone: (08) 9276 6966
Fax: (08) 9200 5839
Email: info@thermomix.com.au
www.thermomix.com.au

Thermomix in New Zealand Trust
Phone: (03) 366 2846
Fax: (03) 366 2064
Email: info@thermomix.co.nz
www.thermomix.co.nz

Managing Director: Grace Mazur

Executive Manager – Marketing and Communications: Jackie Richmond

Managing Editor: Rachel Hanson

Recipe Development and Testing: Kristyn Riccadonna

Print and Digital Content Coordinator: Sarah Bradshaw

Dietitian: Bianca Mazur

Nutritional consultant: Dr. Igor Tabrizian MBBS

Photography: Craig Kinder, f22 Photography

Food styling: Ursula Nairn

Design: Chil3

thermomix

Vegetarian Kitchen

BASICS

BREAKFAST

LIGHT MEALS

MAIN MEALS

DESSERT

INTRODUCTION

Vegetarian diets today look very different from what they were a decade ago. Back then, it was just removing meat from your meals (and it was often replaced with pasta, cheese or other processed foods). Today, it means including more greens, more fibre, more grains and more vitamins and nutrients to benefit your overall health.

We filled this cookbook with flavoursome recipes that also address the importance of providing healthy and nutritious options for vegetarians. By including a wide range of fruits, vegetables, nuts, grains and plant proteins in your diet, you can get all of the nutrients, vitamins and minerals you need. All of the recipes are suited for a lacto-ovo diet (they include eggs and dairy products), but we include tips and variations to adjust recipes to suit a variety of meat-free diets, such as vegan and raw food.

Whether you are looking to reduce your overall intake of meat, celebrate "meatless Mondays" or eliminate meat products from your diet altogether, these recipes will hit all of the flavour notes. You'll even find that the most resolute carnivore will enjoy them!

We hope our recipes inspire you to create your own vegetarian dishes at home. Be sure to share your photos with us on our Facebook, Instagram and Twitter pages!

Grace Mazur

Grace Mazur
Managing Director

INTRODUCTION

Following a vegetarian diet isn't as simple as cutting out meat. When you cut out any food group from your diet, there needs to be careful planning put in place to ensure you are replacing all vitamins and minerals that have been omitted, otherwise you can be at risk of developing nutritional deficiencies. However, there are health benefits associated with following a well-balanced vegetarian diet (or by simply adding more plant-based meals to your current eating plan). This still means you need to follow healthy eating guidelines and base your meals around fruits, vegetables and wholegrains. Like with any diet, it can be easy to reach for convenient and often processed foods – most of which are packed full of sugar, additives, preservatives and unhealthy fats. To help make sure your vegetarian meals are a healthy and nutritious option, make your meals yourself so you can control exactly what is going into them. This way you can also ensure you are getting all those key nutrients that are vital for achieving a nutritionally adequate diet.

Despite the huge range of plant-based foods at our fingertips, some people still believe that vegetarian meals are boring and bland, which definitely is not the case! The Thermomix is a great tool to help you create delicious and nutritious meals for the whole family. This cookbook has a wide variety of yummy vegetarian meals, as well as tips and hints throughout on how to maximise your nutrition.

Bianca Mazur
Dietitian
Executive Manager Group Development

NUTRITION

There are different types of vegetarian diets, which usually exclude meat, chicken and fish but some can also exclude dairy and/or eggs. A vegetarian diet can have many health benefits, as numerous plant foods provide a great source of vitamins, fibre and antioxidants. Vegetarian diets may also help lower the risk of heart disease, cancer, high blood pressure, diabetes and obesity. To achieve these health benefits careful planning needs to go into replacing excluded foods with healthy alternatives that provide similar nutrients. The key to a nutritionally adequate vegetarian diet is consuming a wide variety of foods every day. Throughout this book you will find tips and information on how to best maximise your diet. The following are the main nutrients to be mindful of when you follow a vegetarian diet. Please remember that it is important to seek nutritional advice from a qualified health professional before starting any new eating plan.

Iron

Vegetarian diets can lead to a low iron status, especially in women, as the best source of iron is found in meat. As an alternate iron source, aim to include a variety of the following foods in your diet: eggs, legumes (chickpeas, beans, lentils, soy foods), nuts and dark leafy greens. To help increase the absorption of iron from these foods include a food high in vitamin C with your meal, such as capsicum, tomatoes, strawberries, and citrus fruits. An easy way to achieve this is by adding these high vitamin C foods to a salad served with your high iron meal.

Other tips to assist with your iron levels

- Avoid tea, coffee and wine with your meals as it will decrease your iron absorption.
- Include vitamin A foods in your diet as this will help to release stored iron (i.e. dairy products, sweet potato and carrots).
- Phytate is a compound found in plant foods such as wholegrains, legumes and bran that can reduce the absorption of iron. Soaking and sprouting beans, grains and seeds can reduce the phytate and therefore increase the absorption of iron from these foods.

Protein

It can be relatively easy to have adequate protein in your diet as most foods provide a source of protein. The following foods are good sources to include in your diet: dairy products, eggs, nuts, seeds, wholegrains like quinoa, legumes such as beans, peas, lentils and soy products including tofu. The key is eating a variety of protein sources each day to get a balanced amount in your diet.

Zinc

Zinc is a mineral that is not stored in the body so it is important to obtain adequate amounts on a daily basis. Sources that can be included in a vegetarian diet include: legumes, eggs, dairy products, nuts (especially Brazil nuts, cashews, peanuts), wholegrains, seeds, mushrooms, spinach and broccoli. Soaking and sprouting beans, seeds and grains can help to increase the amount of zinc you absorb from these foods.

Vitamin B12

Vitamin B12 is only naturally found in animal foods. For people who are consuming dairy and eggs, they are good sources to include in your diet. If you are following a vegan diet (only eating foods of plant origin) then you are at risk of vitamin B12 deficiency and may need to eat foods fortified with B12 (such as savoury yeast flakes) or are advised to take a supplement. For further advice on supplementation, please consult with a health professional.

Calcium

If you are including dairy in your diet, aim to consume a variety of dairy products each day. Those who follow a vegan diet are at the highest risk of not consuming enough calcium as the best source is found in dairy products. However, there are many plant-based foods that provide a source of calcium in the diet, such as almonds, tahini (sesame seeds are high in calcium), kale and tofu.

Other tips to assist with your calcium levels

• Avoid high amounts of sodium in your diet as this may cause your body to lose calcium (i.e. avoid large amounts of processed foods which can be quite high in sodium).

• Broccoli and leafy greens, such as spinach, are good sources of calcium, but contain a compound called oxalate which decreases the absorption of calcium from these foods. Try to avoid excessive amounts of these foods in the diet.

• Only consume moderate amounts of caffeine as high amounts can affect calcium absorption and losses in the body.

Omega-3

Eggs are a great source of omega-3 fatty acids. For those people consuming plant-based foods in their diets, alternatives include walnuts, flaxseed, soybeans and tofu.

References

Proc Nutr Soc. 2006 May;65(2):160–8. *Improving the bioavailability of nutrients in plant foods at the household level.* Gibson RS1, Perlas L, Hotz C.

Aust Fam Physician. 2009 Aug;38(8):600–2. *Meeting nutritional needs on a vegetarian diet.* Marsh K1, Zeuschner C, Saunders A, Reid M.

J Am Diet Assoc. *Position of the American Dietetic Association and Dietitians of Canada: Vegetarian diets.* Mangels AR, Messina V, Melina V.

American Journal of clinical nutrition. 2009;89:1627S. *Health effects of vegan diets.* Craig WJ.

SYMBOLS & STANDARDS

Butterfly whisk

Speed soft

Reverse

Dough mode (kneading)

Simmering basket

Varoma Varoma accessory in use

V Vegan

GF Gluten free

NF Nut free

EF Egg free

DF Dairy free

R Raw

Standards

1 AU metric tablespoon (tbsp) = 20 mL
1 AU metric teaspoon (tsp) = 5 mL

Eggs: all eggs used in Thermomix recipes are X-Large (59 g). Using raw egg in Thermomix recipes is at the reader's discretion. Consider alternative recipes that do not require raw eggs, especially when serving to young children, the elderly, pregnant women and those with poor immune systems.

Peeling: unless otherwise stated, all fruits and vegetables are assumed washed and peeled.

Oven temperatures: unless otherwise specified, oven temperatures are for fan-forced ovens. Conventional or gas mark oven conversions will need to be researched before commencing.

Gluten free recipes: to ensure gluten free recipes are gluten free, always read the labels of your products as some may contain traces of wheat or gluten.

BREAKFAST

V GF NF R

DAILY GREEN SMOOTHIE

ACTIVE TIME 10 min | **TOTAL TIME** 10 min | **RECIPE MAKES** 4 portions

INGREDIENTS

130 g Lebanese cucumber,
cut into halves

60 g celery stalks, cut into halves

70 g leafy greens (e.g. baby spinach
or kale leaves)

200 g ice cubes

100 g chilled water

180 g Granny Smith apples (approx. 1–2),
cored and cut into quarters

4 pitted Medjool dates

1 banana (approx.100 g), cut into pieces
(3 cm) and frozen

1 cm cube fresh ginger, peeled

2 tsp chia seeds (optional)

TIPS

Store peeled and chopped banana
pieces in the freezer to make quick
smoothies anytime.

This smoothie is high in iron (from the
leafy greens) and the chia seeds are a
good source of zinc.

PREPARATION

1. Place cucumber, celery, leafy greens, ice cubes and water into mixing bowl and blend **40 sec**/**speed 10**.

2. Add apple, dates, banana, ginger and chia (optional) and blend **2 min**/**speed 8**. Serve immediately.

EVERYDAY PROTEIN SHAKE

ACTIVE TIME 5 min | **TOTAL TIME** 5 min | **RECIPE MAKES** 2 portions

INGREDIENTS

30 g almonds

30 g rolled oats

100 g ice cubes

140 g frozen fruit (e.g. blueberries, strawberries or mango)

1 tbsp honey

1 egg

1 tbsp cold pressed almond oil (optional) (see Tips)

1 tsp green powder, such as spirulina powder (see Tips)

100 g milk of choice (rice, almond, dairy or coconut)

200 g coconut water

TIPS

If you can't find almond oil, you can use other oils such as coconut oil.

You can use any type of powdered superfood blend in this recipe.

If you don't have coconut water, replace it with filtered water.

To make this shake gluten free, simply omit the oats.

Almonds provide both zinc and calcium, which are essential for good health.

PREPARATION

1. Place almonds and oats into mixing bowl and mill **10 sec/speed 9**.

2. Add all remaining ingredients and blend **30 sec/speed 9**.

3. Scrape down sides of mixing bowl with spatula and blend **30 sec/speed 9**, until desired consistency is achieved. Serve immediately.

(EF)

COFFEE AND COCOA TOASTED CEREAL

ACTIVE TIME 15 min | **TOTAL TIME** 50 min | **RECIPE MAKES** 10 portions

INGREDIENTS

1 cinnamon quill

100 g almonds

80 g Brazil nuts

100 g dried figs, cut into halves

1 orange, zest only, no white pith

30 g cocoa powder

250 g rolled oats

½ tsp ground cardamom

80 g brewed espresso coffee

70 g quinoa flakes

70 g pepita seeds

20 g millet

20 g chia seeds

50 g sultanas

60 g dried cranberries

50 g goji berries

60 g shredded coconut

1–2 tsp natural vanilla extract

130 g pure maple syrup

40 g macadamia oil

30–50 g carob pieces

milk of choice, to serve

USEFUL ITEMS

large bowl

baking paper

2 baking trays (30 x 40 cm)

sealable container

PREPARATION

1. Preheat oven to 150°C. Line 2 baking trays (30 × 40 cm) with baking paper and set aside.

2. Place cinnamon quill into mixing bowl and mill **1 min/speed 9**.

3. Add almonds and Brazil nuts and chop **Turbo/1 sec/1 time**.

4. Add figs and orange zest and chop **5 sec/speed 6**.

5. Add cocoa powder, oats, cardamom and brewed coffee and mix **2 min/70°C/↻/speed 2**. Transfer into a large bowl and set aside.

6. Place all remaining ingredients into mixing bowl and mix **2 min/70°C/↻/speed 2**. Transfer into bowl with oat mixture and stir to combine.

7. Spread mixture evenly across prepared baking trays and bake for 30–35 minutes (150°C), or until evenly toasted. Stir mixture 1–2 times during cooking to ensure even cooking.

8. Allow mixture to cool, then transfer into a sealable container or serve immediately with milk.

TIPS

Try serving with yoghurt and fresh fruit.

For stronger chocolate flavour, replace cocoa powder with Dutch cocoa powder.

You can replace the carob with cacao nibs.

Cereal will last in the pantry in a sealable container for up to 2 weeks.

VARIATION

Raw coffee and cocoa cereal:
Set dehydrator to 41°C. Thinly spread mixture on dehydrator sheets and dehydrate for 11 hours (41°C), or until dry and crispy. To dehydrate in an oven, set your oven to its lowest temperature, thinly spread mixture onto baking sheets and dry for 11 hours or until completely dry, stirring once or twice during drying time. Transfer into a sealable container or serve immediately.

GF EF

PEAR BERRY CEREAL

ACTIVE TIME 10 min | **TOTAL TIME** 10 min | **RECIPE MAKES** 4 portions

INGREDIENTS

100 g pear, cored and cut into eighths

30 g raw almonds

30 g hazelnuts

20 g pumpkin seeds

20 g sunflower seeds

30 g shredded coconut

40 g dried apricots

2 tsp pure maple syrup

½ tsp ground cinnamon

50 g organic puffed rice (white or brown)

100 g Greek yoghurt, to serve

100 g fresh mixed berries
(e.g. strawberries, blueberries,
raspberries), to serve

2 tbsp carob pieces, to serve (optional)

PREPARATION

1. Place pears, almonds, hazelnuts, pumpkin seeds, sunflower seeds, coconut, apricots, syrup and cinnamon into mixing bowl and pulse **Turbo/1 sec/2 times**, or until roughly chopped.

2. Add puffed rice and combine **20 sec/↺/speed 3**, with aid of spatula.

3. Serve with yoghurt, fresh mixed berries and carob pieces (optional).

TIPS

This cereal is best eaten on the day it's made.

To make just 2 portions, simply divide all ingredients in half and pulse **Turbo/1 sec/1 time** in step 1. Proceed as per recipe.

To save time, weigh seeds, nuts, coconut and cinnamon in advance and store in a container. In the morning, proceed as per recipe.

GF **EF**

ORANGE AND MANGO CHIA PUDDING

ACTIVE TIME 15 min | **TOTAL TIME** 3 hour 15 min | **RECIPE MAKES** 8 portions

INGREDIENTS

Chia pudding

1 orange, flesh only, deseeded and cut into quarters

6 fresh mint leaves

350 g fresh mango cheeks, cut into pieces (2–3 cm)

400 g coconut milk

½ tsp ground cardamom

1 tbsp pure maple syrup

100 g chia seeds

Topping

50 g macadamia nuts

50 g raw almonds

50 g shredded coconut

¼–½ tsp ground cinnamon

2 tsp coconut oil

120–150 g fresh passionfruit pulp, to serve

100–150 g Greek yoghurt, to serve

USEFUL ITEMS

plastic wrap

8 serving glasses

sealable container

PREPARATION

Chia pudding

1. Place orange, mint and 150 g of the mango into mixing bowl and chop **10 sec/speed 7**. Scrape down sides of mixing bowl with spatula.

2. Add all remaining pudding ingredients, except remaining mango, and combine **3 sec/speed 5**. Divide mixture between 8 serving glasses or small sealable jars and place into refrigerator for 5 minutes to firm. Layer puddings with remaining 200 g mango pieces. Cover with plastic wrap or jar lids and place into refrigerator for a minimum of 2 hours (see Tips). Clean and dry mixing bowl.

Topping

3. Place macadamias and almonds into mixing bowl and chop **1 sec/speed 6**, or until roughly chopped.

4. Add coconut, cinnamon and coconut oil and cook **5 min/50°C/↺/speed 1**. Allow to cool completely, then transfer into a sealable container until ready to use.

5. Remove puddings from refrigerator, spoon 1–2 teaspoons passionfruit pulp over each pudding, top with 1–2 tablespoons yoghurt and sprinkle with nut topping to serve.

TIPS

You can replace the fresh mango with frozen, defrosted mango and fresh passionfruit pulp with canned or jarred passionfruit pulp.

The chia seeds and nuts provide zinc, and the yoghurt and almonds are sources of calcium and protein.

These puddings are a great "on the go" breakfast option. You can make the pudding the night before (through step 2) and store in sealable jars or containers in the refrigerator overnight. Simply add the toppings in the morning before you leave the house.

NF **EF**

FRUIT SCONES

ACTIVE TIME 10 min | TOTAL TIME 30 min | RECIPE MAKES 8 portions

INGREDIENTS

280 g wholemeal self-raising flour, plus extra for dusting

60 g goji berries

60 g dried apricots, cut into halves

60 g pitted Medjool dates

40 g light brown sugar

1 tsp ground cinnamon

½ tsp bicarbonate of soda

¼ tsp salt

100 g unsalted butter, cut into pieces (2 cm), plus extra to serve

160 g Greek yoghurt

USEFUL ITEMS

baking tray (20 × 30 cm)

baking paper

bowl

PREPARATION

1. Preheat oven to 200°C. Line a baking tray (20 × 30 cm) with baking paper. Lightly dust with flour and set aside.

2. Place goji berries, apricots and dates into mixing bowl and chop **3 sec/speed 5**. Transfer into a bowl and set aside.

3. Place flour, sugar, cinnamon, bicarbonate of soda, salt and butter into mixing bowl and mix **5 sec/speed 6**.

4. Add yoghurt and reserved fruit and knead **12 sec/**. Transfer dough onto prepared baking tray. Dust dough with extra flour and gently shape into a large circle (approx. 20 cm diameter). Using the spatula, cut dough into 8 wedges. Separate wedges (approx. 1 cm apart) and bake for 14–16 minutes (200°C), or until golden. Serve warm with butter.

GF DF

FENNEL, DATE AND NUT BREAD

ACTIVE TIME 25 min | TOTAL TIME 1 hour 15 min | RECIPE MAKES 10 slices

INGREDIENTS

Nut paste

55 g macadamia oil (see Tips)

400 g raw almonds

100 g pumpkin seeds

100 g sunflower seeds

60 g sesame seeds

2 pinches sea salt, to taste

1 tbsp caster sugar (optional)

Bread

oil, for greasing

120 g pitted Medjool dates

70 g dried figs, cut into halves

1 tsp fennel seeds

4 eggs

1 tsp bicarbonate of soda

1 tbsp apple cider vinegar

slivered almonds, for garnishing (optional)

USEFUL ITEMS

jug

sealable storage jar or container

loaf tin (18 × 7 × 6 cm)

baking paper

wooden skewer

wire rack

PREPARATION

Nut paste

1. Place a jug onto the mixing bowl lid and weigh macadamia oil into it, then set aside.

2. Place 250 g of the almonds into mixing bowl and mill **10 sec/speed 8**. Scrape down sides of mixing bowl with spatula.

3. Add pumpkin seeds, sunflower seeds, sesame seeds, sea salt, caster sugar (optional) and remaining 150 g almonds into mixing bowl and mix **40 sec/speed 8**.

4. Scrape down sides of mixing bowl with spatula and mix **1 min/speed 4**, slowly pouring oil onto mixing bowl lid, letting it trickle into mixing bowl to emulsify until a paste consistency is achieved. Mix for a further **1 min/speed 8**, with aid of spatula.

5. Transfer into a sealable storage jar or container and set aside. Clean and dry mixing bowl.

Bread

6. Preheat oven to 150°C. Grease and line a loaf tin (18 × 7 × 6 cm) with baking paper and set aside.

7. Place dates, figs and fennel seeds into mixing bowl and chop **15 sec/speed 8**.

8. Add eggs, bicarbonate of soda, vinegar and 370 g of the reserved nut paste into mixing bowl and blend **10 sec/speed 5**.

9. Transfer mixture into prepared tin and sprinkle with slivered almonds (optional).

10. Bake for 40–50 minutes (150°C), or until a wooden skewer inserted into the centre of the loaf comes out clean.

11. Allow to cool in tin, then transfer onto a wire rack to cool completely before serving.

TIPS

You can replace the macadamia oil with grapeseed oil.

Leftover nut paste must be stored in the refrigerator for up to 2 weeks.

You can store this loaf in a sealable container for up to 3 days, or store in the freezer (wrapped in foil) for up to 2 months.

This recipe provides protein, calcium and zinc and other nutrients, such as vitamin E and essential fatty acids.

NF

ASPARAGUS AND PEA OMELETTE

ACTIVE TIME 20 min | **TOTAL TIME** 20 min | **RECIPE MAKES** 2 portions

INGREDIENTS

40 g Gruyère cheese, cut into pieces
(3 cm) (optional)

3 spring onions/shallots (approx. 70 g),
trimmed and cut into pieces (3–4 cm)

1 garlic clove

1 tsp soy sauce

½ tsp sesame oil

1 tsp sesame seeds

80 g fresh green peas (see Tips)

6 stalks asparagus, trimmed and cut
into halves

6 eggs

1–2 pinches sea salt, to season

1–2 pinches ground black pepper,
to season

1–2 tsp grapeseed oil, for frying

1–2 sprigs fresh coriander, leaves only,
for garnishing

USEFUL ITEMS

bowl

serving plates

kitchen towel

frying pan

PREPARATION

1. Place cheese (optional) into mixing bowl and grate **5 sec/speed 9**. Transfer into a bowl and set aside. Clean and dry mixing bowl.

2. Place spring onions/shallots and garlic into mixing bowl and chop **3 sec/speed 7**. Scrape down sides of mixing bowl with spatula.

3. Add soy sauce, sesame oil and sesame seeds and cook **2 min/100°C/speed 1**.

4. Add peas and asparagus and cook **2–4 min/100°C/⟲/speed 1**, or until asparagus is tender. Transfer into a bowl and set aside. Rinse mixing bowl.

5. Crack eggs into mixing bowl, season with salt and pepper and blend **6 sec/speed 6**.

6. Place a small frying pan (19 cm) over medium heat and add 1 teaspoon oil. Pour half of the egg mixture into pan and swirl to coat base of pan. Cook for 1–2 minutes, or until just cooked. Spread half of the reserved pea and asparagus mixture over half of the omelette and top with half of the reserved cheese (optional). Fold omelette over to enclose filling and cook for a further 1-2 minutes, or until cooked through. Transfer onto a serving plate and cover to keep warm.

7. Repeat with remaining half of the egg and filling mixtures.

8. Garnish with coriander before serving.

TIPS

You can use frozen peas in this recipe, simply thaw before using in step 4.

To make this recipe dairy free, omit the cheese.

Eggs are a source of both protein and vitamin B12.

Varoma **NF**

VEGETABLE BAKE WITH GOAT'S FETA

ACTIVE TIME 25 min | **TOTAL TIME** 1 hour 30 min | **RECIPE MAKES** 6 portions

INGREDIENTS

Lemon chilli dressing

4 pieces lemon peel (1 × 5 cm), no white pith

1 long red chilli, deseeded if preferred

3 sprigs fresh lemon thyme, leaves only

1 garlic clove

40 g extra virgin olive oil

20 g lemon juice

Vegetable bake

olive oil, for greasing

1–2 Ruby Lou potatoes, peeled and cut into very thin slices (see Tips)

2 garlic cloves

300 g sweet potato, cut into pieces (4–5 cm)

200 g carrot, cut into pieces (4–5 cm)

100 g zucchini, cut into pieces (4–5 cm)

40 g cornflour

80 g red onion, cut into thin strips

80 g red capsicum, deseeded and cut into thin strips

1 egg

½ tsp salt

½ tsp freshly ground black pepper

150 g Swiss brown mushrooms, cut into slices

30 g fresh baby spinach leaves, to serve

70 g goat's milk feta, crumbled, to serve

USEFUL ITEMS

bowl

baking tray (30 × 40 cm)

large bowl

PREPARATION

Lemon chilli dressing

1. Place lemon peel, chilli, lemon thyme and garlic into mixing bowl and chop **3 sec**/**speed 7**. Scrape down sides of mixing bowl with spatula.

2. Add oil and heat **3 min**/**Varoma**/**speed 1**.

3. Add lemon juice and mix **3 sec**/**speed 2**. Transfer into a bowl and set aside. Clean and dry mixing bowl.

Vegetable bake

4. Preheat oven to 180°C. Thoroughly grease a baking tray (30 × 40 cm, with rimmed edges).

5. Place a thin layer of Ruby Lou potatoes over base of baking tray. Bake for 10 minutes (180°C), then set aside.

6. Place garlic and sweet potato into mixing bowl and grate **3 sec**/**speed 5**. Transfer into a large bowl.

7. Place carrot and zucchini into mixing bowl and chop **3 sec**/**speed 5**. Transfer into bowl with sweet potato.

8. Place large bowl onto mixing bowl lid and weigh cornflour, onion and capsicum into it. Add egg, salt, pepper and reserved lemon chilli dressing into bowl and stir to combine. Spread mixture evenly over potato base and bake for 40 minutes (180°C).

9. Place mushrooms on top of vegetable mixture and bake for a further 10–15 minutes (180°C), or until top is golden and sides are crispy around the edges.

10. Top vegetable bake with spinach leaves and sprinkle with crumbled feta to serve.

TIPS

Use a mandolin slicer to easily cut potato into thin slices.

You can replace goat's feta with Greek or Australian feta in this recipe.

For a protein boost, try serving with poached eggs. You can find the recipe in *The Basic Cookbook* or *Everyday Cookbook*.

You can make this in a large baking dish; you will have a crispier result with a thinly spread mixture.

(V) (NF)

TOFU SCRAMBLE

ACTIVE TIME 25 min | **TOTAL TIME** 25 min | **RECIPE MAKES** 4 portions

INGREDIENTS

6 spring onions/shallots (approx. 100 g), trimmed and cut into quarters

1 garlic clove

¼ tsp mustard powder

¼ tsp ground turmeric

¼ tsp ground cumin

¼ tsp dried thyme

¼ tsp salt, plus extra to serve

¼ tsp ground black pepper, plus extra to serve

1 tbsp olive oil

2 tbsp water

70 g red capsicum, deseeded and cut into pieces (1 cm)

70 g fresh corn kernels (see Tips)

350 g firm tofu, cut into cubes (2 cm)

30 g fresh baby spinach leaves, cut or torn into pieces

6 sprigs fresh chives, cut into thin slices

20 g lemon juice, to taste

4 slices rye bread, toasted, to serve

1 avocado, flesh only, cut into slices, to serve

PREPARATION

1. Place spring onions/shallots and garlic into mixing bowl and chop **3 sec**/**speed 7**. Scrape down sides of mixing bowl with spatula.

2. Add mustard powder, turmeric, cumin, thyme, salt, pepper, oil and water and cook **3 min**/**100°C**/**speed 1**.

3. Add capsicum, corn and tofu and cook **4 min**/**80°C**/⟳/**speed 1**.

4. Add spinach, chives and lemon juice. Mix well using spatula and cook **2 min**/**80°C**/**speed** ⟲.

5. Serve immediately on rye toast with avocado slices and season with extra salt and pepper.

TIPS

You can replace fresh corn with thawed frozen corn.

Include this recipe as part of a big breakfast, served with *Baked beans* (see pg. 34) and/or *Breakfast sausages* (see pg. 36).

This dish is a powerhouse of nutrition providing iron, zinc, calcium, protein and vitamin C to aid iron absorption.

GF NF EF

STUFFED PORTOBELLO MUSHROOMS

ACTIVE TIME 15 min | **TOTAL TIME** 1 hour | **RECIPE MAKES** 6 portions

INGREDIENTS

Polenta

6 fresh Portobello mushrooms

240 g water

220 g full cream milk

2 tsp olive oil

2 dried bay leaves

½ tsp dried thyme

1 tbsp Vegetable stock paste (see Tips)

100 g polenta (see Tips)

1–2 pinches sea salt, to taste

½ tsp ground black pepper, to taste

100 g mascarpone cheese

Caramelised onion and Brussels sprouts

8 Brussels sprouts, cut into halves

1 garlic clove

120 g red onion, cut into halves

20 g unsalted butter

1 tbsp soft dark brown sugar

1 tbsp balsamic vinegar

½ tsp sea salt

USEFUL ITEMS

baking tray (30 × 40 cm)

baking paper

bowl

PREPARATION

Polenta

1. Preheat oven to 180ºC. Line a baking tray (30 × 40 cm) with baking paper.

2. Remove stalks from mushrooms and discard. Place mushrooms onto prepared tray, gill side up. If any of the mushrooms do not sit flat, remove a small slice from the bottom of the mushroom. Set baking tray with mushrooms aside.

3. Place water, milk, oil, bay leaves, thyme and stock paste into mixing bowl and cook **5 min/90ºC/speed 1**. Carefully remove bay leaves and discard.

4. Add polenta, salt and pepper and cook **15 min/100ºC/speed 4**. Scrape down sides of mixing bowl with spatula, then set mixture aside in mixing bowl to cool for approx. 10 minutes.

5. Add mascarpone and mix **10 sec/speed 2**.

6. Transfer polenta into reserved mushrooms to fill, then bake for 20 minutes (180ºC). Clean and dry mixing bowl. Meanwhile, continue with Caramelised onion and Brussels sprouts.

Caramelised onion and Brussels sprouts

7. Place Brussels sprouts into mixing bowl and chop **3 sec/speed 5**. Transfer into a bowl and set aside.

8. Place garlic and onion into mixing bowl and chop **3 sec/speed 5**. Scrape down sides of mixing bowl with spatula.

9. Add all remaining ingredients, except Brussels sprouts, and cook **8 min/Varoma/↺/speed ⋌**.

10. Add reserved Brussels sprouts and cook **2 min/Varoma/↺/speed ⋌**.

11. Garnish mushrooms with caramelised onions and Brussels sprouts before serving.

TIPS

Refer to *The Basic Cookbook* or *Everyday Cookbook* for the Vegetable stock paste recipe.

We suggest using fine polenta in this reicpe, do not use the quick-cooking variety.

BAKED BEANS

ACTIVE TIME 10 min | **TOTAL TIME** 13 hour 25 min | **RECIPE MAKES** 4 portions

INGREDIENTS

380 g dried navy beans (see Tips)

1700 g water

1 brown onion (approx. 150 g), cut into halves

1 garlic clove

1 long red chilli, deseeded if preferred

1 tsp dried basil

30 g extra virgin olive oil

5 cm piece kombu (optional) (see Glossary, pg. 178)

1 tbsp apple juice concentrate

2 tsp molasses

1½ tbsp Vegetable stock paste (see Tips)

1 tsp tamari

½ tsp seeded mustard

400 g canned tomatoes

USEFUL ITEMS

ceramic or glass bowl

sealable container

PREPARATION

1. Place a ceramic or glass bowl onto mixing bowl lid and weigh navy beans and 850 g of the water into it. Set aside to soak overnight.

2. Drain beans through simmering basket, rinse and set aside.

3. Place onion, garlic, chilli and basil into mixing bowl and chop **3 sec/speed 7**. Scrape down sides of mixing bowl with spatula.

4. Add oil and cook **2 min/100°C/speed 1**.

5. Add kombu (optional), apple juice concentrate, molasses, stock paste, tamari, mustard, reserved beans and remaining 850 g water and cook **45 min/Varoma/↻/speed ⦚**.

6. Add tomatoes and cook **30 min/100°C/↻/speed ⦚**, or until beans are cooked.

7. Serve immediately or transfer into a sealable container, allow to cool, then place into refrigerator until ready to serve.

TIPS

You can find navy beans at health food stores or dried goods stores. You can replace the navy beans with dried cannellini beans.

You can replace dried beans with canned beans in this recipe (see Glossary, pg. 178), however be sure to rinse and drain the canned beans prior to cooking. Omit Steps 1 and 2, begin recipe from Step 3.

Please refer to *The Basic Cookbook* or *Everyday Cookbook* for the Vegetable stock paste recipe.

Serve on sourdough toast, or as part of a hearty breakfast.

You can freeze any leftovers.

Beans are high in fibre, iron and protein, and the tomatoes are high in vitamin C and help increase the amount of iron your body can absorb.

To aid with digestion and reduce flatulence caused by the fibre in the beans, you may want to add a small amount (just a pinch or two) of asafoetida (see Glossary, pg. 178) during step 3. You can buy asafoetida at Indian food stores, some Asian food stores, health food stores and online.

BREAKFAST SAUSAGES

ACTIVE TIME 35 min | **TOTAL TIME** 1 hour 5 min | **RECIPE MAKES** 6 portions (2–3 pieces each)

INGREDIENTS

Rice

1200 g water
200 g brown rice

Vegetable sausages

150 g rolled oats
50 g fresh mushrooms
200 g firm tofu, cut into pieces (2–3 cm)
50 g zucchini, cut into pieces (2–3 cm)
100 g brown onion, cut into quarters
80 g semi sun-dried tomatoes, drained
¼ tsp sea salt
¼ tsp ground black pepper
2 tbsp soy sauce
2 sprigs fresh rosemary, leaves only
5 sprigs fresh flat-leaf parsley, leaves only
10 sprigs fresh sage, leaves only
1 tsp fennel seeds
1 tbsp savoury yeast flakes (see Tips)
1 tsp xanthan gum (see Tips)
2–4 tbsp oil, for frying
tomato sauce, to serve

USEFUL ITEMS

bowl
large non-stick frying pan
thermal serving bowl (ThermoServer) or plate

PREPARATION

Rice

1. Place water into mixing bowl. Insert simmering basket and weigh brown rice into it. Cook **30 min/100°C/speed 4**. Remove simmering basket with aid of spatula and set aside to cool. Clean and dry mixing bowl.

Vegetable sausages

2. Place oats into mixing bowl and mill **5 sec/speed 7**. Transfer into a bowl and set aside.

3. Place mushrooms, tofu, zucchini, onion, sun-dried tomatoes, salt, pepper, soy sauce, rosemary, parsley, sage, fennel seeds, savoury yeast flakes, xanthan gum, reserved cooked rice and 100 g of the milled oats into mixing bowl. Chop **30–40 sec/speed 9**, with aid of spatula until mixture is well combined.

4. Using damp hands, roll 2 tablespoons of the sausage mixture into a sausage shape. Roll sausage in remaining 50 g milled oats to coat and set aside. Repeat process to create approx. 14 sausages.

5. Place a large non-stick frying pan over medium heat and add 1–2 tablespoons of the oil. Add sausages to pan in batches and cook for 5-10 minutes, turning occasionally until lightly golden all over. Transfer into a thermal serving bowl (ThermoServer) or onto a large plate and cover to keep warm. Add more oil if needed and cook remaining sausages. Serve immediately with tomato sauce.

TIPS

You can find xanthan gum in the health food aisle in most supermarkets, health food stores or online.

To save time in the morning, cook the rice the night before.

To make your own tomato sauce, please refer to the recipe in *The Basic Cookbook* or *Everyday Cookbook*.

Savoury yeast flakes are often fortified with vitamin B12 (be sure to check the label). You can buy them at most health food stores.

Varoma **NF** **DF**

SPICED FENNEL AND SILVERBEET WITH FRIED EGGS

ACTIVE TIME 15 min | **TOTAL TIME** 35 min | **RECIPE MAKES** 4 portions

INGREDIENTS

200 g fresh silverbeet (approx. 1 bunch), stalks removed, leaves cut into strips (2–3 cm)

200 g fennel bulb, trimmed and cut into thin slices (1–2 mm)

4 spring onions/shallots (approx. 70 g), trimmed and cut into quarters

2 garlic cloves

1½ tsp sumac

2 star anise

1 tbsp soy sauce

2 tbsp avocado oil

500 g water

250 g truss cherry tomatoes

1 tbsp pumpkin seeds, to serve (optional)

1 tbsp sunflower seeds, to serve (optional)

4 eggs, fried, to serve

ground black pepper, to season

USEFUL ITEMS

baking paper

serving plates

PREPARATION

1. Line Varoma dish with a piece of wet, well-wrung baking paper. Place Varoma into position, then weigh silverbeet and fennel into it. Set Varoma aside.

2. Place spring onions/shallots and garlic into mixing bowl and chop **3 sec/speed 5**. Scrape down sides of mixing bowl with spatula.

3. Add sumac, star anise, soy sauce and oil and cook **2 min/100°C/speed 1**. Carefully pour hot mixture over silverbeet and fennel.

4. Without cleaning mixing bowl, place water into mixing bowl. Place Varoma into position, secure Varoma lid and steam **8 min/Varoma/speed 1**.

5. Stir silverbeet and fennel, place Varoma tray into position and place truss tomatoes onto Varoma tray. Steam **2–3 min/Varoma/speed 1**, or until tomatoes are cooked to your liking.

6. Set Varoma aside and remove baking paper to allow excess liquid to drain. Remove and discard star anise.

7. Divide silverbeet mixture between 4 plates, top with pumpkin and sunflowers seeds (optional), fried eggs and season with pepper. Serve with tomatoes on the side.

TIPS

You can replace the avocado oil with grapeseed oil, or other lightly flavoured oil in this recipe.

To make this recipe suitable for a vegan diet, simply omit the eggs.

The silverbeet provides iron and calcium, while the eggs add protein and vitamin B12 to your meal.

LIGHT MEALS

(GF) (NF) (DF) (R)

AVOCADO SORBET (PALATE CLEANSER)

ACTIVE TIME 10 min | **TOTAL TIME** 10 min | **RECIPE MAKES** 8 portions

INGREDIENTS

150 g sugar

1 avocado (approx. 120 g), flesh only, cut into pieces

700 g ice

1 egg white

TIPS

To make this recipe egg free and vegan, omit egg white in step 3. Proceed as per recipe.

This palate cleanser is ideal to serve between entree and main at a dinner party.

PREPARATION

1. Place sugar into mixing bowl and mill **10 sec**/**speed 10**. Scrape down sides of mixing bowl with spatula.

2. Add avocado and 350 g of the ice and blend **30 sec**/**speed 10**, with aid of spatula.

3. Add egg white and remaining 350 g ice and blend **1–2 min**/**speed 10**, or until ice is completely crushed. Serve immediately or place into freezer until ready to serve.

V GF R

BASIL SORBET (PALATE CLEANSER)

ACTIVE TIME 10 min | **TOTAL TIME** 10 min | **RECIPE MAKES** 8 portions

INGREDIENTS

130–150 g caster sugar, to taste

60 g pine nuts

170 g lemons (approx. 2), skin thoroughly washed, ends trimmed, deseeded and cut into quarters (see Tips)

20 g fresh basil leaves (approx. 1–2 bunches) (see Tips)

700 g ice cubes

50–100 g water

USEFUL ITEMS

serving bowl

TIPS

If possible, use organic lemons as there will be little to no waxy residue on the skin.

When adding the basil in step 2, be sure to place into mixing bowl in handfuls so the scales are able to sense the weight.

This palate cleanser is ideal to serve between entree and main at a dinner party.

PREPARATION

1. Place sugar and 40 g of the pine nuts into mixing bowl and chop **10 sec/speed 10**.

2. Add lemons, basil and ice and blend **1 min/speed 1**, **increasing speed gradually from speed 1 to speed 8**, with aid of spatula.

3. Scrape down sides of mixing bowl with spatula. Add 50 g of the water and blend **1 min 30 sec/speed 7**, with aid of spatula, adding extra water as needed, until a smooth consistency is achieved.

4. Transfer into a serving bowl and garnish with remaining 20 g pine nuts. Serve immediately or place into freezer until ready to serve.

EF

CRISPY BREAD WITH TAPENADE

ACTIVE TIME 20 min | **TOTAL TIME** 45 min | **RECIPE MAKES** 6 portions

INGREDIENTS

1 wholemeal bread loaf, cut into slices and crusts removed

extra virgin olive oil (approx. 1 tsp per slice of bread)

100 g cheddar cheese, cut into pieces (3 cm)

30 g capers, drained

3 garlic cloves

100 g roasted pine nuts

60 g pitted Kalamata olives

2–3 sprigs fresh basil, leaves only, for garnishing

USEFUL ITEMS

2 baking trays (30 × 40 cm)

baking paper

rolling pin

serving bowl

PREPARATION

1. Preheat oven to 200°C. Line 2 baking trays (30 × 40 cm) with baking paper and set aside.

2. Flatten each bread slice with a rolling pin and cut into quarters diagonally (to create 4 triangles). Drizzle generously with oil (approx. 1 teaspoon per slice). Transfer bread pieces onto prepared trays and bake for 20–25 minutes (200°C) until crispy. Set aside to cool.

3. Place cheese, capers, garlic, pine nuts and olives into mixing bowl and blend **10 sec**/**speed 7**. Transfer into a serving bowl and garnish with basil leaves. Serve tapenade with crispy bread.

TIPS

Transfer tapenade into a sealable jar or container and store in refrigerator until ready to serve.

For extra flavour, drizzle with *Basil oil* (see pg. 100).

LINSEED CRACKERS WITH MUTABBAL BEITINJAN (EGGPLANT DIP)

ACTIVE TIME 20 min | **TOTAL TIME** 16 hour 20 min | **RECIPE MAKES** 4 portions

INGREDIENTS

Mutabbal beitinjan (eggplant dip)

1 eggplant (approx. 400 g), cut into halves lengthways and skin pricked all over with a fork

3 garlic cloves, unpeeled

50 g olive oil, plus extra for drizzling

1 tbsp lemon juice

½ tsp sea salt, to taste

1–2 pinches ground black pepper, to taste

40 g pitted Kalamata olives

1 tsp ground cumin

3 sprigs fresh flat-leaf parsley, leaves only

20 g tahini (see Tips)

30 g natural yoghurt

Flaxseed (linseed) crackers

230 g flaxseeds (linseeds)

30 g brown onion

1 garlic clove

100 g red capsicum, deseeded and cut into quarters

100 g green capsicum, deseeded and cut into quarters

400 g tomatoes, cut into quarters

4 sun-dried tomatoes, drained

250 g water, room temperature

2 tsp dried Italian herbs blend

½ tsp sea salt, to taste

pomegranate arils, for garnishing

USEFUL ITEMS

baking tray (30 × 40 cm)

baking paper

large bowl

plastic wrap

sealable container

3 baking trays or dehydrator sheets

PREPARATION

Mutabbal beitinjan (eggplant dip)

1. Preheat oven to 200°C. Line a baking tray (30 × 40 cm) with baking paper.

2. Place eggplant and garlic onto prepared baking tray and drizzle with a little of the extra oil. Bake for 20–30 minutes (200°C), turning once after approx. 10 minutes, until eggplant is soft.

3. Transfer into a large bowl and cover with plastic wrap for 10 minutes. Peel off blackened skin and discard.

4. Place eggplant, garlic and all remaining ingredients, into mixing bowl and chop **30 sec/speed 5**. Scrape down sides of mixing bowl with spatula.

5. **Insert butterfly whisk**. Blend **1 min/speed 4**. Season to taste. **Remove butterfly whisk**. Transfer into a sealable container and place into refrigerator until ready to serve. Clean and dry mixing bowl.

Flaxseed (linseed) crackers

6. Place flaxseeds (linseeds) into mixing bowl and mill **10 sec/speed 9**. Transfer into a bowl and set aside.

7. Place onion, garlic, capsicums, tomatoes and sun-dried tomatoes into mixing bowl and blend **30 sec/speed 7**. Scrape down sides of mixing bowl with spatula.

8. Add water, Italian herbs and salt and mix **20 sec/speed 5**.

9. Add reserved milled flaxseeds (linseeds) and mix **20 sec/speed 1**, or until combined.

10. Thinly spread mixture onto dehydrator sheets and dehydrate for approx. 12 hours (41°C). If drying in the oven, preheat oven to 100°C and line 3 baking trays with baking paper. Divide mixture between baking trays and spread out thinly. Bake for 3 hours (100°C). Remove from oven, carefully peel biscuits off baking paper, turn over and bake for a further 30 minutes (100°C). Turn off oven and allow cracker to dry out in the oven overnight.

11. Allow to cool completely before breaking into pieces. Serve with eggplant dip garnished with pomegranate arils.

TIPS

To make your own *Tahini*, see pg. 124.

If using the dehydrator method, the crackers are suitable for those following a raw food diet.

This cracker recipe can also be used as a raw flat bread or raw pizza base.

You can store crackers in a sealable container for 2–3 days.

This recipe provides calcium, protein, iron, B vitamins, omega-3 and vitamin C.

Go to the Thermomix in Australia YouTube channel to watch a video on how to easily remove the arils from your pomegranate in the Thermomix.

NF EF

OATCAKES WITH MOROCCAN HOMMUS

ACTIVE TIME 20 min | **TOTAL TIME** 50 min | **RECIPE MAKES** 6 portions

INGREDIENTS

Oatcakes

30 g unsalted butter, cut into pieces (4–5 cm)

70 g water

½ tsp sea salt

1 tbsp raw sugar

180 g oats

¼ tsp bicarbonate of soda

Harissa

150 g fresh red chillies, cut into pieces

600 g boiling water

2½ tsp cumin seeds

2 tsp coriander seeds

5 garlic cloves

40 g extra virgin olive oil

1 tsp salt

Moroccan hommus

2 garlic cloves

2 tbsp extra virgin olive oil

400 g canned chickpeas, rinsed and drained (approx. 250 g after draining)

2 tbsp water

2 tbsp lime juice (approx. 1 lime)

1 tbsp tahini (see Tips)

½ tsp sea salt

USEFUL ITEMS

2 baking trays (30 × 40 cm)

baking paper

silicone bread mat (ThermoMat)

rolling pin

round cookie cutter (5 cm)

ceramic or glass bowl

sealable storage jar or container

PREPARATION

Oatcakes

1. Preheat oven to 190°C. Line 2 baking trays (30 × 40 cm) with baking paper and set aside.

2. Place butter, water, salt and sugar into mixing bowl and heat **3 min/90°C/speed 3**.

3. Add oats and bicarbonate of soda and mix **10 sec/speed 5**, until a crumbly dough forms.

4. Transfer dough onto a silicone bread mat (ThermoMat) or lightly floured work surface and shape dough with hands. Place a sheet of baking paper on top of dough and roll out thinly (2 mm). Using a cookie cutter (5 cm), cut dough into 30 rounds and place onto prepared trays.

5. Bake for 12–14 minutes (190°C), or until crisp. Turn off oven and allow oatcakes to cool in oven. Clean and dry mixing bowl.

Harissa

6. Place a ceramic or glass bowl onto mixing bowl lid and weigh chillies and boiling water into it. Soak chillies in boiling water (approx. 10 minutes), then drain using simmering basket and set aside.

7. Place cumin and coriander seeds into mixing bowl and dry roast **4 min/100°C/speed 1**.

8. Allow to cool for 5 minutes, then mill **3 sec/speed 9**.

9. Add garlic and chop **3 sec/speed 7**. Scrape down sides of mixing bowl with spatula.

10. Add 20 g of the oil and cook **2 min/100°C/speed 1**.

11. Add salt, reserved chillies and remaining 20 g oil and blend **30 sec/speed 8**. Transfer into a sealable jar or container and place into refrigerator until ready to use. Clean and dry mixing bowl.

Moroccan hommus

12. Place garlic into mixing bowl and chop **3 sec/speed 7**. Scrape down sides of mixing bowl with spatula.

TIPS

To make your own *Tahini*, see pg. 124.

Harissa is a spicy chilli paste from North Africa. Adjust the amount of chillies you use to suit your taste. Store harissa in a sealable jar or container in the refrigerator. Use in sauces, marinades or dips to add extra spice and flavour.

Leftover harissa can be stored in the refrigerator for up to 1 month.

Substitute fresh chillies with dried chillies in the harissa. Soak dried chillies in water for 1 hour, then drain and proceed as per recipe.

To make these oatcakes suitable for those following a vegan diet, replace butter with oil of choice.

For the hommus, you can replace the lime juice with lemon juice. For a thicker consistency, replace the citrus juice with water.

You can replace canned chickpeas with dried chickpeas (soaked and cooked) in this recipe (see pg. 179).

To aid with digestion, you may want to add a small amount (just a pinch or two) of asafoetida (see Glossary, pg. 178) during step 13. You can buy asafoetida at Indian food stores, some Asian food stores, health food stores and online.

13. Add oil and cook **1 min**/**Varoma**/**speed 1**.

14. Add 2–3 teaspoons of the reserved harissa and cook **1 min**/**Varoma**/**speed 1**.

15. Add chickpeas, water and lime juice and mix **30 sec**/**speed 5**. Scrape down sides of mixing bowl with spatula.

16. Add tahini and salt and blend **10 sec**/**speed 6**, until smooth. Transfer into a serving bowl and serve with oatcakes.

BROAD BEAN BRUSCHETTA

ACTIVE TIME 10 min | **TOTAL TIME** 30 min | **RECIPE MAKES** 4 portions

INGREDIENTS

50 g Parmesan cheese, crust removed and cut into pieces (3 cm)

1000 g water

500 g frozen broad beans, thawed

50 g frozen green peas

2 garlic cloves

2 sprigs fresh basil, leaves only

2 spring onions/shallots, trimmed and cut into quarters

10 pimento-stuffed olives

2 tsp lemon juice (approx. ½ lemon)

1–2 pinches sea salt, to taste

1–2 pinches ground black pepper, to taste

1 sourdough bread loaf, cut into slices (2 cm thick) and toasted

100 g feta cheese, crumbled

1 tbsp extra virgin olive oil, for garnishing (optional)

1 lemon, zest only, no white pith, for garnishing (optional)

USEFUL ITEMS

small bowl

PREPARATION

1. Place Parmesan cheese into mixing bowl and grate **10 sec/speed 8**. Transfer into small bowl and set aside.

2. Place water into mixing bowl, insert simmering basket and weigh beans and peas into it and cook **12–15 min/Varoma/speed 1**, or until tender and cooked.

3. Remove simmering basket with aid of spatula and set aside to cool. Once beans have cooled, remove and discard outer pods and set beans aside. Discard water in mixing bowl.

4. Place 1 of the garlic cloves, basil and spring onions/shallots into mixing bowl and chop **3 sec/speed 7**. Scrape down sides of mixing bowl with spatula.

5. Add olives, lemon juice, salt, pepper, half of the reserved beans and peas and all of the reserved Parmesan, then blend **5 sec/speed 4**.

6. Add remaining half of the beans and peas and combine **5 sec/⮌/speed 3**.

7. Cut remaining garlic clove into pieces and rub over toasted sourdough slices. Thickly spread each slice with broad bean mixture, top with feta and garnish with oil (optional) and lemon zest (optional) before serving.

TIPS

When in season, use fresh broad beans instead of frozen ones.

The beans and cheese in this recipe provide calcium and protein.

EF

GORGONZOLA PANNA COTTA WITH PEAR AND WALNUT SALAD

ACTIVE TIME 25 min | TOTAL TIME 3 hour 55 min | RECIPE MAKES 6 portions

INGREDIENTS

Gorgonzola panna cotta

90 g gorgonzola, cut into pieces (2 cm)

400 g full cream milk

300 g pouring (whipping) cream

¾ tsp agar agar powder (see Tips)

Pear and walnut salad

30 g macadamia oil

1 tbsp lemon juice

1 tsp Dijon mustard

2 pinches sea salt, to taste

2 pinches ground black pepper, to taste

100 g mixed salad greens

1 pear, cut into halves, cored and cut into thin slices

50 g walnuts

USEFUL ITEMS

bowl

6 dariole moulds (120 mL)

plastic wrap

sealable bottle

large bowl

PREPARATION

Gorgonzola panna cotta

1. Place a bowl onto mixing bowl lid and weigh gorgonzola into it. Set aside.

2. Place milk and cream into mixing bowl and cook **5 min/37°C/speed 2**.

3. Add agar agar powder and cook **9 min/90°C/speed 4**.

4. Mix **2 min/90°C/speed 2**, slowly adding gorgonzola through hole in mixing bowl lid, until combined. Divide mixture between six dariole moulds (120 ml) and allow to cool at room temperature for approx. 30 minutes. Cover with plastic wrap, then place into refrigerator for a minimum of 3 hours or overnight until set. Clean and dry mixing bowl.

Pear and walnut salad

5. Place macadamia oil, lemon juice, mustard, salt and pepper into mixing bowl and mix **25 sec/speed 5**. Transfer into a sealable bottle and set aside.

6. Place mixed salad greens, pear and walnuts into a large bowl and gently toss to combine.

7. Remove panna cottas from refrigerator. Using a butter knife, gently remove panna cottas from moulds and turn out onto serving plates. Serve with salad and a drizzle of reserved dressing.

TIPS

Leftover dressing can be stored in the refrigerator for up to 1 week.

Agar agar yields the best results when combined with hot liquids, then transferred into the refrigerator to set.

You can find agar agar powder at health food stores, some Asian food stores and online.

EF **DF**

RICE PAPER ROLLS WITH SWEET AND SOUR CHILLI SAUCE

ACTIVE TIME 40 min | **TOTAL TIME** 40 min | **RECIPE MAKES** 10 pieces

INGREDIENTS

Sweet and sour chilli sauce

1 lime, zest only, no white pith

1–1½ fresh red chillies, deseeded if preferred, to taste

1 garlic clove

½ tsp ground black pepper

2 cm piece fresh ginger, peeled

20 g lime juice

3 sprigs fresh mint, leaves only

3 sprigs fresh coriander, leaves and roots only

80 g pineapple, cut into pieces

70 g tomato

20 g honey

20 g tamari

1 pinch sea salt

Rice paper rolls

100 g carrot, cut into quarters

1 red apple, cored and cut into halves

180 g red cabbage, cut into pieces (6–8 cm)

8 sprigs fresh coriander, leaves and stalks only

2 tbsp roasted salted peanuts

1 avocado, flesh only

2–3 pinches salt

2–3 pinches ground black pepper

10 sheets rice paper wrappers (see Tips)

½ yellow peach, stone removed and flesh cut into thin slices

2 sprigs fresh mint, leaves only

1 Lebanese cucumber, peeled into ribbons

USEFUL ITEMS

sealable storage jar or container

serving platter

PREPARATION

Sweet and sour chilli sauce

1. Place lime zest, chillies, garlic, pepper and ginger into mixing bowl and blend **10 sec/speed 8**. Scrape down sides of mixing bowl with spatula.

2. Add all remaining sauce ingredients and purée **1 min/speed 10**. Transfer into a sealable jar or container and place into refrigerator until ready to serve. Clean and dry mixing bowl.

Rice paper rolls

3. Place carrot, apple, cabbage, coriander stalks, peanuts, avocado, salt and pepper into mixing bowl and chop **2 sec/speed 4**.

4. Scrape down sides and bottom of mixing bowl with spatula and chop **2 sec/speed 4**.

5. Prepare rice paper wrappers as per packet instructions.

6. Place 1 wrapper onto a clean work surface. Arrange 2–3 peach slices, 1 mint leaf, 1–2 coriander leaves and 2 cucumber ribbons down the centre of the wrapper. Place 2 tablespoons of the cabbage mixture on top of cucumber.

7. Fold in left and right sides of wrapper, then fold up bottom of wrapper over filling and roll away from you to completely enclose filling. Place seam side down onto a serving platter. Continue with remaining wrappers and filling to create 10 rolls. Serve cold with sweet and sour chilli sauce.

TIPS

Leftover sauce can be stored in the refrigerator for up to 2 weeks.

You can buy rice paper rolls at major supermarkets and Asian grocers.

If peaches aren't available, you could use nectarines or pears.

To make this recipe suitable for those following a raw food diet, replace roasted peanuts with raw nuts of choice.

Varoma

CAULIFLOWER AND FENNEL NUGGETS WITH AJVAR

ACTIVE TIME 30 min | TOTAL TIME 1 hour 35 min | RECIPE MAKES 35 pieces

INGREDIENTS

Ajvar (capsicum and eggplant dip)

2 red capsicums (approx. 420 g), cut into halves and deseeded

1 eggplant (approx. 350 g), cut into halves lengthways

40 g olive oil, plus extra for drizzling

1 garlic clove

1 fresh red chilli, deseeded if preferred

6 pitted Kalamata olives

4 sprigs fresh flat-leaf parsley, leaves only

2 pinches salt

2 pinches ground smoked paprika

20 g lemon juice

Cauliflower and fennel nuggets

500 g water

150 g cauliflower florets

150 g fennel bulb, trimmed and cut into slices

100 g cheddar cheese, cut into pieces (3–4 cm)

3 spring onions/shallots (approx. 60 g), trimmed and cut into quarters

2 sprigs fresh flat-leaf parsley, leaves only, plus extra (optional) to serve

1 garlic clove

20 g olive oil

100 g breadcrumbs

1 tsp Dijon mustard

1 egg

1 tsp salt

1 tsp freshly ground black pepper

2 tsp savoury yeast flakes

40 g pine nuts

lemon, cut into wedges, to serve (optional)

PREPARATION

Ajvar (capsicum and eggplant dip)

1. Preheat oven to 200°C. Line a baking tray (30 × 40 cm) with baking paper.

2. Place capsicum and eggplant, skin side up, onto baking tray. Drizzle with a little oil and bake for 30 minutes (200°C).

3. Transfer eggplant and capsicum into a large bowl and cover with plastic wrap to steam for 10 minutes. Peel off skins and discard.

4. Place garlic, chilli, olives and parsley into mixing bowl and chop **3 sec/speed 5**. Scrape down sides of mixing bowl with spatula.

5. Add oil, salt, paprika, lemon juice and reserved capsicum and eggplant, then chop **5 sec/speed 4**.

6. Scrape down sides of mixing bowl with spatula and cook **3–6 min/Varoma/↻/speed ⚊**, placing simmering basket instead of measuring cup onto mixing bowl lid, until mixture thickens.

7. Transfer into a sealable container, allow to cool to room temperature, then place into refrigerator until ready to serve. Clean and dry mixing bowl.

Cauliflower and fennel nuggets

8. Line a baking tray (30 × 40 cm) with baking paper and set aside.

9. Place water into mixing bowl, place Varoma into position and weigh cauliflower and fennel into it. Secure Varoma lid and steam **10 min/Varoma/speed 2**. Set Varoma aside and discard water. Dry mixing bowl.

10. Place cooked cauliflower and fennel into mixing bowl and chop **5 sec/↻/speed 5**. Transfer into a bowl and set aside.

11. Place cheese into mixing bowl and grate **8 sec/speed 7**. Transfer into bowl with cauliflower and set aside.

12. Place spring onions/shallots, parsley, garlic and oil into mixing bowl and chop **5 sec/speed 7**.

13. Scrape down sides of mixing bowl with spatula, then sauté **3 min/100°C/speed 1**.

14. Add remaining ingredients, excluding lemon wedges, including reserved cauliflower and cheese, and mix **10 sec/↻/speed 4**.

USEFUL ITEMS

baking tray (30 × 40 cm)

baking paper

large bowl

plastic wrap

sealable container

bowl

TIP

Ajvar is a Serbian relish or side dish, popular in the Balkan region of Southeast Europe.

15. Shape 1 tablespoon of the cauliflower mixture into a cylinder shape, then place onto prepared baking tray. Repeat with remaining mixture to make approx. 35 nuggets, washing your hands occasionally to prevent mixture from sticking to your hands.

16. Bake for 12–15 minutes (200°C), or until golden. Serve nuggets warm with ajvar, lemon wedges (optional) and parsley (optional).

EF

NACHOS WITH BEANS AND CASHEW SOUR CREAM

ACTIVE TIME 30 min | TOTAL TIME 50 min | RECIPE MAKES 4 portions

INGREDIENTS

Cashew sour cream

3 sprigs fresh chives, cut into quarters

1 garlic clove

120 g raw cashew nuts

150 g water

1 tsp sea salt

60 g brown onion

40 g lemon juice (approx. 1 lemon)

Black bean hommus

1 garlic clove

400 g canned black beans, rinsed and drained (approx. 250 g after draining)

60 g lemon juice (approx. 2 lemons)

30 g tahini (see Tips)

1 tsp ground cumin

2 pinches sea salt, to taste

2 pinches ground cayenne pepper

1 tsp paprika

40 g pitted Kalamata olives

Tomato and kidney bean sauce

1 brown onion (approx. 150 g), cut into halves

2 garlic cloves

30 g unsalted butter

¼–½ tsp dried chilli flakes, to taste

1 tsp ground cumin

1 tsp ground coriander

2 tsp ground paprika

400 g canned tomatoes

60 g tomato paste

1 tbsp dark brown sugar

420 g canned kidney beans, rinsed and drained (approx. 250 g after draining

Nachos

180 g cheddar cheese, cut into pieces (3 cm)

20 g Parmesan cheese, crust removed and cut into pieces (3 cm)

340 g corn chips

PREPARATION

Cashew sour cream

1. Place chives and garlic into mixing bowl and chop **5 sec/speed 7**. Transfer into a bowl and set aside.

2. Place all remaining sour cream ingredients into mixing bowl and blend **20 sec/speed 9**. Scrape down sides of mixing bowl with spatula.

3. Cook **5 min/90°C/speed 3**, then blend **30 sec/speed 9**, until smooth.

4. Add reserved chive mixture and stir **5 sec/speed 3**.

5. Transfer into a sealable jar or container, allow to cool to room temperature then place into refrigerator until ready to serve. Clean and dry mixing bowl.

Black bean hommus

6. Place all hommus ingredients into mixing bowl and mix **15 sec/speed 7**.

7. Transfer hommus into a sealable jar or container and place into refrigerator until ready to serve. Clean and dry mixing bowl.

Tomato and kidney bean sauce

8. Place onion and garlic into mixing bowl and chop **5 sec/speed 7**.

9. Add butter and sauté **3 min/100°C/speed 1**.

10. Add all remaining ingredients, except kidney beans, and cook **3 min/100°C/speed 1**.

11. Add kidney beans and cook **1 min/90°C/⟲/speed 1**, then chop **4 sec/speed 2**. Transfer into a bowl and set aside. Clean and dry mixing bowl.

Nachos

12. Preheat oven to 180°C. Grease a casserole dish (30 × 25 cm) and set aside.

13. Place cheeses into mixing bowl and grate **10 sec/speed 8**. Transfer into a bowl and set aside.

14. Layer half of the corn chips into base of prepared casserole dish. Spread with half of the reserved kidney bean mixture and sprinkle with half of the reserved cheese mixture. Repeat layering with remaining chips, kidney bean mixture and cheese mixture. Bake for 15–20 minutes (180°C), or until golden brown. Serve hot with black bean hommus and cashew sour cream.

USEFUL ITEMS

bowl

sealable storage jar or container

casserole dish (30 × 25 cm)

TIPS

To make your own *Tahini*, see pg. 124.

You can also serve these nachos with guacamole (refer to the recipe in *The Basic Cookbook* or *Everyday Cookbook*) and lime wedges.

This recipe provides a number of essential nutrients, including iron, calcium, zinc and vitamin C, as well as protein.

You can replace canned beans with dried beans (soaked and cooked) in this recipe (see pg. 179).

To aid with digestion and reduce flatulence caused by the fibre in the beans, you may want to add a small amount (just a pinch or two) of asafoetida (see Glossary, pg. 178) during cooking. You can buy asafoetida at Indian food stores, some Asian food stores, health food stores and online.

(NF)

CORN AND CORIANDER FRITTERS WITH AVOCADO TAHINI

ACTIVE TIME 20 min | **TOTAL TIME** 1 hour 15 min | **RECIPE MAKES** 4 portions

INGREDIENTS

Avocado tahini

1 avocado, flesh only

2 tbsp tahini (see Tips)

20 g lime juice (approx. 1 lime)

2 tbsp extra virgin olive oil

1 pinch salt, to taste

1 pinch ground black pepper, to taste

Corn and coriander fritters

3 spring onions/shallots (approx. 60 g), cut into quarters

10 sprigs fresh coriander, leaves only

100 g kale, leaves only, stalks removed

140 g natural yoghurt

2 eggs

110 g self-raising flour

½ tsp salt, to taste

½ tsp freshly ground black pepper, to taste

500 g fresh corn kernels (see Tips)

2 pinches cayenne pepper

oil, for frying

USEFUL ITEMS

serving bowl

bowl

large frying pan

thermal serving bowl (ThermoServer) or plate

PREPARATION

Avocado tahini

1. Place all avocado tahini ingredients into mixing bowl and blend **5 sec**/**speed 5**.

2. Scrape down sides of mixing bowl with spatula and mix **3 sec**/**speed 5**. Transfer into a serving bowl and place into refrigerator until ready to serve. Do not clean mixing bowl.

Corn and coriander fritters

3. Place spring onions/shallots, coriander and kale into mixing bowl and chop **3 sec**/**speed 7**, with aid of spatula.

4. Scrape down sides of mixing bowl with spatula and chop **3 sec**/**speed 7**. Transfer into a bowl and set aside.

5. Place yoghurt, eggs, flour, salt and pepper into mixing bowl and mix **10 sec**/**speed 5**.

6. Add corn, cayenne pepper and reserved spring onion/shallot mixture and mix **20 sec**/↺/**speed 3**, until combined.

7. Place a large frying pan over medium heat and brush with oil. Working in batches, pour 2 tablespoons of the fritter mixture into pan and cook for approx. 3 minutes on each side or until golden and cooked through. Transfer into a thermal serving bowl (ThermoServer) or onto a plate and cover to keep warm. Repeat with remaining fritter mixture to make approx. 16 fritters total. Serve fritters with reserved avocado tahini.

TIPS

To make your own *Tahini*, see pg. 124.

You can replace the fresh corn with thawed frozen corn in this recipe.

NF **EF**

CHILLI CHUTNEY QUESADILLAS

ACTIVE TIME 20 min | **TOTAL TIME** 1 hr | **RECIPE MAKES** 4 portions

INGREDIENTS

Chilli chutney

500 g brown onion, cut into eighths, layers separated

1 apple, peeled, cored and cut into eighths

1 red capsicum, deseeded and cut into thin strips (1 cm)

2 tbsp brown sugar

40 g unsalted butter, cut into pieces (1–2 cm)

¼ tsp sea salt

2 tbsp balsamic vinegar

1 tsp dried chilli flakes

Quesadilla

8 multigrain tortillas

16 Swiss cheese slices

50–80 g baby spinach leaves

USEFUL ITEMS

bowl

sandwich press

PREPARATION

Chilli chutney

1. Place all chutney ingredients into mixing bowl and cook **10 min/Varoma/speed** ↺.

2. Cook for a further **10 min/Varoma/speed** ↺, **without measuring cup**.

3. **Insert measuring cup**. Mix **10 sec/speed 4**. Transfer chutney into a bowl and set aside to cool (approx. 15 minutes).

Quesadilla

4. Preheat a sandwich press (see Tips).

5. Place 4 tortillas onto a clean work surface. Place 1 cheese slice onto one half of each tortilla. Evenly divide half of the reserved chutney between tortillas and spread onto one half of each tortilla. Divide half of the spinach between tortillas to cover chutney, then top each half with 1 cheese slice. Fold over remaining half of tortilla to encase filling.

6. Cook each tortilla in sandwich press for 3–5 minutes, or until cheese has melted. Carefully transfer quesadilla onto a serving plate and cover to keep warm. Repeat with remaining quesadillas. Cut into wedges before serving.

TIPS

If you do not have a sandwich press, you can cook quesadillas on your stove top. In step 6, place a frying pan over medium heat. Place 1 quesadilla into the pan and cook for 2–3 minutes. Carefully flip over and cook for a further 2–3 minutes, or until cheese has melted. Transfer to a serving plate and cover to keep warm. Repeat with remaining quesadillas.

To make a more complete meal, serve with a green salad or coleslaw.

Varoma V

SWEETCORN AND BLACK RICE SALAD

ACTIVE TIME 15 min | **TOTAL TIME** 1 hr | **RECIPE MAKES** 4 portions

INGREDIENTS

Dressing

80 g light olive oil

30 g orange juice (approx. ½ orange)

30 g apple cider vinegar

1 tsp Dijon mustard

2 pinches salt, to taste

2 pinches ground black pepper, to taste

Black rice salad

200 g black rice (see Tips)

1000 g water

2 cinnamon quills

1 tsp caraway seeds

5 cardamom pods, crushed

2 sweet corn cobs, husk removed

1 orange, peeled and segmented

1 pomegranate, cut into quarters and arils removed (see Tips)

5 sprigs fresh coriander, leaves only, cut into pieces

5 sprigs fresh mint, leaves only, cut into pieces

10 sprigs fresh flat-leaf parsley, leaves only, cut into pieces

20–40 g red onion, cut into thin slices

100 g pecans

USEFUL ITEMS

sealable bottle

baking tray (30 × 40 cm)

PREPARATION

Dressing

1. Place all dressing ingredients into mixing bowl and combine **3 sec/speed 5**. Season to taste, transfer into a bottle and set aside until ready to serve.

Black rice salad

2. Insert simmering basket, then weigh rice into it. Remove simmering basket with aid of spatula and rinse rice until water runs clear. Place water into mixing bowl, then re-insert simmering basket with rice.

3. Add cinnamon, caraway seeds and cardamom pods into simmering basket. Place Varoma into position and place corn cobs into it. Secure Varoma lid and cook **22 min/100°C/speed 4**. Set Varoma aside to allow corn to cool (approx. 10 minutes). Remove kernels from cob and set aside. Discard cobs.

4. Continue to cook rice **4–6 min/100°C/speed 4**, or until cooked to your liking.

5. Remove simmering basket with aid of spatula, transfer rice onto a baking tray (30 × 40 cm) and spread out to allow rice to cool (approx. 15 minutes). Discard cinnamon quills and cardamom pods. Clean and dry mixing bowl.

6. Transfer all remaining salad ingredients, including cooled rice and corn, into a large bowl (see Tips). Drizzle with a little dressing and gently toss to combine. Serve immediately or place into refrigerator until ready to serve.

TIPS

All components of the salad can be made in advance and stored in the refrigerator. Simply assemble and dress salad, as per step 6, just before serving.

Go to the Thermomix in Australia YouTube channel to learn how to easily remove your pomegranate arils in your Thermomix.

You can buy black rice at most major supermarkets.

Leftover dressing can be stored in the refrigerator for up to 1 week.

Varoma **GF** **EF**

"SPAGHETTI" WITH SPINACH AND MINT PESTO

ACTIVE TIME 30 min | **TOTAL TIME** 45 min | **RECIPE MAKES** 4 portions

INGREDIENTS

Spinach and mint pesto

50 g extra virgin olive oil

1½ tbsp lime juice

200 g fresh baby spinach leaves

8 sprigs fresh mint, leaves only

50 g shelled salted pistachios

1 garlic clove

¼ tsp salt

Carrot and zucchini "spaghetti"

500 g water

1–2 zucchinis (approx. 200 g), peeled into "spaghetti" (see Tips)

1–2 carrots (approx. 200 g), peeled into "spaghetti" (see Tips)

100 g sugar snap peas, cut into thin strips

Parmesan cheese, shaved, to serve

freshly ground black pepper, to serve

USEFUL ITEMS

jug

bowl

serving bowls

PREPARATION

Spinach and mint pesto

1. Place a jug onto mixing bowl lid and weigh oil and lime juice into it, then set aside.

2. Place 100 g of the spinach into mixing bowl and chop **3 sec**/**speed 5**. Scrape down sides of mixing bowl with spatula.

3. Add mint, pistachios, garlic, salt and remaining 100 g spinach into mixing bowl and chop **10 sec**/**speed 5** with aid of spatula.

4. Scrape down sides of mixing bowl with spatula and mix **1 min**/**speed 4**, slowly pouring oil mixture onto mixing bowl lid letting it trickle into mixing bowl, until combined. Transfer into a bowl and place into refrigerator until ready to serve. Clean and dry mixing bowl.

Carrot and zucchini "spaghetti"

5. Place water into mixing bowl. Place Varoma dish into position, then place zucchini and carrots into it. Secure Varoma lid and steam **6–8 min**/**Varoma**/**speed 1**, or until tender. Transfer zucchini and carrots into a large serving bowl.

6. Add sugar snap peas to serving bowl and toss to combine. Transfer into serving bowls and top with reserved pesto. Garnish with Parmesan cheese and pepper before serving.

TIPS

We recommend using a vegetable peeler with a spiral or "spaghetti" attachment to peel zucchini and carrot. Alternatively, peel vegetables and cut into very thin strips.

This recipe is a good source of both iron and calcium.

FATTOUSH SALAD WITH GRILLED HALOUMI

ACTIVE TIME 20 min | **TOTAL TIME** 3 hr 20 min | **RECIPE MAKES** 4 portions

INGREDIENTS

Haloumi

2000 g full cream milk

4 junket tablets (see Tips)

250 g water, plus extra for dissolving

20 g salt

Salad dressing

1 garlic clove

60 g extra virgin olive oil

40 g lemon juice (approx. 1 lemon), plus extra for serving

1–2 tsp sumac, to taste

¼ tsp sugar (optional)

Fattoush

2 pita breads

2 tbsp extra virgin olive oil, for brushing and frying

2 Lebanese cucumbers (approx. 235 g), cut into halves, deseeded and cut into pieces (2 cm)

1 red capsicum (approx. 225 g), cut into halves, deseeded and cut into pieces (2 cm)

1 green capsicum (approx. 180 g), cut into halves, deseeded and cut into pieces (2 cm)

½ red onion, cut into thin slices

4 red radishes, cut into halves, then cut into thin slices

200 g cherry tomato, cut into halves

7 sprigs fresh flat-leaf parsley, leaves only, torn into pieces

7 sprigs fresh coriander, leaves only, torn into pieces

1–2 pinches sea salt, to taste

1–2 pinches ground black pepper, to taste

PREPARATION

Haloumi

1. To set curds, place milk into mixing bowl and heat **10 min/37°C/speed 1**.

2. Place junket tablets and 1 tbsp water into a separate bowl and stir to combine.

3. Add junket mixture into mixing bowl and combine **1 min/speed 1**. Transfer milk into a thermal serving bowl (ThermoServer) or other large bowl, cover and set aside for 1 hour. Clean and dry mixing bowl.

4. Cut curds into strips (2 cm) each way at a 45° angle. Allow to sit for another 10 minutes for curds and whey to develop further.

5. Place curds and whey into mixing bowl and heat **30 min/37°C/speed ⟲**.

6. Place simmering basket over a jug and line simmering basket with cheese cloth. Transfer curds and whey into cheese cloth. Fold overhanging cheese cloth over curds and whey to cover. Place a heavy weight (such as a can of beans) on top of curds and whey. Set aside for 30 minutes to allow whey to drain. Clean and dry mixing bowl.

7. Place whey from jug into mixing bowl and heat **5 min/90°C/speed 1**.

8. Remove curds from cheese cloth and cut into slices (1 cm thick). Discard cheese cloth and place curds back into simmering basket. Insert simmering basket into mixing bowl and cook **30 min/90°C/speed ⟲**, or until haloumi pieces rise to the top of the liquid.

9. Set simmering basket aside and allow haloumi to cool.

10. Transfer whey into a jug and set aside.

11. Place water and salt into mixing bowl and heat for **3 min/100°C/speed 1**.

12. Add 250 g of the reserved whey and cook **5 min/100°C/speed 1**. Transfer into a sealable container and set aside to cool. Discard excess whey.

13. Add haloumi to cooled brine mixture and place into refrigerator until ready to serve. Clean and dry mixing bowl.

Continued on page 70

Continued from page 68

Salad dressing

14. Place garlic into mixing bowl and chop **3 sec/speed 7**. Scrape down sides of mixing bowl with spatula.

15. Add all remaining salad dressing ingredients and mix **10 sec/speed 6**. Transfer into a jug and set aside until ready to serve.

Fattoush

16. Preheat oven grill. Place pita breads onto baking tray (30 × 40 cm) and toast both sides for 1–2 minutes each, until puffed and starting to crisp. Carefully remove baking tray from grill, slice pita breads into halves horizontally and open into 4 separate pieces. Brush with a little oil, return to grill and toast the inside until golden brown (approx. 1 minute). Carefully tear into bite-size pieces and set aside to cool.

17. Place cucumber, capsicums, onion, radish, cherry tomato and herbs into a large bowl. Add pita pieces and reserved dressing and stir to combine. Season to taste with salt and pepper, then divide between 4 serving plates.

18. Drain haloumi and pat dry. Place a frying pan over medium-high heat and add oil. Fry haloumi until golden (approx. 1–2 minutes each side).

19. Arrange over salad and drizzle with extra lemon juice, if desired. Serve immediately.

TIPS

Junket tablets contain rennet, which helps form milk curds to make cheese. You can buy junket tablets at most major supermarkets.

You can store haloumi in the refrigerator for 1–2 weeks in the brine mixture. The longer it is soaked in the brine, the saltier it will taste.

This dish is a good source of both vitamin C (used for iron absorption) and calcium.

POLISH CROQUETTES WITH MUSHROOM AND SAUERKRAUT

ACTIVE TIME 10 min | **TOTAL TIME** 1 hr 20 min | **RECIPE MAKES** 4 portions

INGREDIENTS

Crêpe mixture

330 g water

230 g full cream milk

2 eggs

20 g grapeseed oil

310 g plain flour

1 pinch sea salt

Filling

500 g sauerkraut

1000 g water

1 tbsp oil, plus extra for frying

1 brown onion (approx. 150 g), cut into halves

500 g button mushrooms, cut into halves

1½ tsp sea salt, to taste

1–1½ tsp ground black pepper, to taste

120 g breadcrumbs, for coating

2 tbsp butter, for frying

USEFUL ITEMS

bowl

large frying pan (26 cm)

large plate

frying pan (19 cm)

silicone bread mat (ThermoMat)

PREPARATION

Crêpe mixture

1. Place all crêpe ingredients into mixing bowl and mix **20 sec/speed 5**.

2. Scrape down sides of mixing bowl with spatula and mix **5 sec/speed 5**. Transfer into a bowl and set aside for 20 minutes. Clean and dry mixing bowl.

Filling

3. Place sauerkraut into simmering basket and gently rinse under running water. Set aside.

4. Place water into mixing bowl. Insert simmering basket with sauerkraut and cook **12 min/Varoma/speed 1**. Remove simmering basket with aid of spatula, then set aside to drain and cool. Clean and dry mixing bowl.

5. Place a large frying pan (26 cm) over medium heat and add 1 tablespoon of the oil.

6. Place onion into mixing bowl and chop **3 sec/speed 5**. Transfer into frying pan.

7. Place half of the mushrooms into mixing bowl and chop **2 sec/speed 4**. Transfer into frying pan.

8. Place remaining mushrooms into mixing bowl and chop **2 sec/speed 4**. Transfer into frying pan.

9. Place drained sauerkraut into mixing bowl and chop **2 sec/speed 7**. Transfer into frying pan.

10. Add salt and pepper to frying pan and stir until liquid in pan has nearly evaporated (approx. 10–15 minutes). Transfer mushroom mixture into a bowl and allow to cool (approx. 5 minutes).

11. Place a large plate onto mixing bowl lid and weigh breadcrumbs onto it. Set aside.

Continued on page 72

Continued from page 71

12. Place a frying pan (19 cm) over medium heat and add a little oil. Using a measuring cup, pour ⅓ cup of reserved crêpe mixture into pan and swirl to cover base. Cook for 1–2 minutes, or until edges start to lift away from pan. Flip uncooked side of crêpe onto the plate containing breadcrumbs. Gently press down, allowing breadcrumbs to coat crêpe completely. Transfer onto a separate plate. Repeat with remaining crêpe mixture to make a total of 8 crêpes.

13. Place 1 crêpe, breadcrumb side down, onto a silicone bread mat (ThermoMat) or clean work surface. Place 3 tablespoons of mushroom mixture into the centre of the crêpe. Fold left and right sides of crêpe inwards (approx. 2 cm) to enclose filling. Roll crêpe up from the bottom to the top, to fully enclose filling, creating a croquette shape. Repeat with remaining crêpes and mushroom filling.

14. Place frying pan (19 cm) over medium heat and add butter. Cook croquettes in batches for 1–2 minutes on each side until golden brown all over. Serve immediately.

TIPS

These croquettes are traditionally served with a bowl red clear borscht (see pg. 86).

You can also serve these with a garden salad.

The sauerkraut in this recipe provides vitamin C (which aids in iron absorption), and the fermentation enhances the availability of the nutrients in the sauerkraut.

Varoma ▦ **V**

ISRAELI COUSCOUS SALAD

ACTIVE TIME 20 min | **TOTAL TIME** 1 hr | **RECIPE MAKES** 4 portions

INGREDIENTS

Dressing

3 garlic cloves

60 g extra virgin olive oil, plus extra to taste

50 g red onion, cut into halves

1 tsp dried oregano

½ tsp ground cumin

½ tsp ground cinnamon

½ tsp ground ginger

⅛ tsp ground cayenne pepper

1 tsp grated lemon zest, no white pith

40 g lemon juice, plus extra to taste

3 sprigs fresh mint, leaves only, torn into pieces

3 sprigs fresh flat-leaf parsley, leaves only, torn into pieces

3 sprigs fresh basil, leaves only, torn into pieces

Couscous salad

800 g water

200 g Israeli couscous, rinsed and drained (also known as pearl couscous)

200 g red lentils, rinsed and drained

200 g broccoli florets (2 cm)

200 g cauliflower florets (2 cm)

250 g cherry tomatoes, cut into halves

100 g pitted Kalamata olives, cut into halves

30 g pine nuts

40 g pistachio nuts

40 g slivered almonds

1–2 pinches sea salt, to taste

1–2 pinches ground black pepper, to taste

USEFUL ITEMS

bowl

large bowl

PREPARATION

Dressing

1. Place garlic into mixing bowl and chop **3 sec**/**speed 7**. Scrape down sides of mixing bowl with spatula.

2. Add oil and cook **1 min 30 sec**/**100°C**/**speed 1**.

3. Add onion, oregano, cumin, cinnamon, ginger, cayenne, lemon zest and juice and chop **3 sec**/**speed 7**. Scrape down sides of mixing bowl with spatula.

4. Add remaining herbs and combine **10 sec**/↻/**speed 2**. Transfer into a bowl and set aside.

Couscous salad

5. Without cleaning mixing bowl, place water into mixing bowl. Insert simmering basket, then weigh couscous and lentils into it. Place Varoma dish into position and weigh broccoli and cauliflower into it. Secure Varoma lid and steam **9 min**/**Varoma**/**speed 2**.

6. Set Varoma aside and stir couscous and lentils, then stir broccoli and cauliflower. Place Varoma back into position and secure Varoma lid, then cook **2–4 min**/**Varoma**/**speed 2**, or until lentils and couscous are cooked to your liking.

7. Remove Varoma. Remove simmering basket with aid of spatula and rinse couscous and lentils under cold water. Set aside to drain. Rinse broccoli and cauliflower under cold water and set aside to drain.

8. Transfer drained ingredients into a large bowl and place onto mixing bowl lid. Weigh all remaining salad ingredients, including reserved dressing into bowl. Add extra oil, lemon juice, salt and pepper to taste. Place into refrigerator until ready to serve.

TIPS

This salad is a good source of all the essentials: iron, vitamin C, calcium, zinc and protein.

Israeli (or pearl) couscous is larger than standard couscous and can be found in most major supermarkets in the pasta aisle.

MASHED PEA AND CORN SLICE

ACTIVE TIME 5 min | **TOTAL TIME** 40 min | **RECIPE MAKES** 6 portions

INGREDIENTS

Mashed pea and corn slice

butter, for greasing

3 spring onions/shallots (approx. 90 g), trimmed and cut into quarters

3 sprigs fresh basil, leaves only

100 g tasty cheese, cut into pieces (3–4 cm)

500 g frozen green peas, thawed

400 g canned chickpeas, drained and rinsed (approx. 250 g after draining)

250 g frozen corn kernels, thawed

4 eggs

2 tsp seeded mustard

50 g plain flour

½ tsp baking powder

1 tsp salt

½ tsp ground black pepper, to taste

Green goddess dressing

3 pieces lemon zest, no white pith (1 × 5 cm)

1 garlic clove

100 g fresh baby spinach leaves

7 sprigs fresh flat-leaf parsley, leaves only

20 sprigs fresh chives, cut into quarters

1 tbsp dried tarragon

50 g mayonnaise (see Tips)

50 g sour cream

2 tbsp lemon juice

1 pinch sumac (optional)

1 spring onion/shallot, trimmed and cut into quarters

USEFUL ITEMS

baking dish (30 × 20 cm)

baking paper

sealable storage jar or container

serving bowl

PREPARATION

Mashed pea and corn slice

1. Preheat oven to 200°C. Grease and line a baking dish (30 × 20 cm) with baking paper and set aside.

2. Place spring onions/shallots, basil, cheese and 250 g of the peas into mixing bowl and chop **3 sec/speed 7**. Scrape down sides of mixing bowl with spatula.

3. Add all remaining slice ingredients, including remaining peas, and mix **10 sec/↺/speed 4**, with aid of spatula. Transfer mixture into prepared baking dish and bake for 30–35 minutes (200°C), or until set and golden in colour. Clean and dry mixing bowl.

Green goddess dressing

4. Place lemon zest and garlic into mixing bowl and chop **10 sec/speed 7**. Scrape down sides of mixing bowl with spatula.

5. Add all remaining dressing ingredients and blend **30 sec/speed 5**. Transfer into a serving bowl or a sealable jar or container until ready to serve.

6. Serve slice hot or cold with green goddess dressing.

TIPS

Use leftover dressing on greens salads or pasta salads, or serve over scrambled eggs with sourdough toast.

The chickpeas and cheese provide protein, and the spinach is a source of iron.

To make your own mayonnaise, please refer to the recipe in *The Basic Cookbook* or *Everyday Cookbook*.

You can replace canned chickpeas with dried chickpeas (soaked and cooked) in this recipe (see pg. 179).

Varoma **V**

SOBA NOODLE AND TOFU SALAD

ACTIVE TIME 20 min | **TOTAL TIME** 35 min | **RECIPE MAKES** 4 portions

INGREDIENTS

Dressing

2 cm piece fresh ginger

6 sprigs fresh mint, leaves only

6 sprigs fresh coriander, roots and stalks (leaves reserved for garnishing)

40 g rice wine vinegar

40 g pure maple syrup

40 g tamari

1 tbsp tahini (see Tips)

40 g extra virgin olive oil

2 tsp miso paste

2 tsp sesame oil

200 g extra firm tofu, cut into pieces (1 cm thick × 2–3 cm length)

Salad

1600 g water

200 g frozen edamame beans

200 g dried soba noodles

1 carrot (approx. 100 g), cut into matchsticks

1 fresh Lebanese cucumber (approx. 100 g), cut into halves lengthways, deseeded and thinly sliced

2 spring onions/shallots, trimmed and cut into thin slices

80 g snow peas, cut into thin slices

1 fresh chilli, cut into thin slices

USEFUL ITEMS

large bowl

bowl

PREPARATION

Dressing

1. Place all ingredients, except tofu, into mixing bowl and mix **5 sec/speed 9**.

2. Scrape down sides of mixing bowl with spatula and mix **10 sec/speed 4**.

3. Transfer dressing into a large bowl, add sliced tofu and stir to combine. Set aside. Rinse mixing bowl.

Salad

4. Place water into mixing bowl, place Varoma dish into position and weigh edamame beans into it. Secure Varoma lid and cook **12 min/Varoma/speed 1**. Remove Varoma and stir edamame.

5. Add soba noodles to mixing bowl, place Varoma back into position and cook **3 min/100°C/↺/speed 1**. Transfer edamame into a bowl and set aside to cool. Once cooled, remove beans from pods and discard pods. Set beans aside.

6. Transfer noodles into Varoma dish and rinse under cold water to cease cooking. Set aside to drain.

7. Transfer drained noodles into large bowl with dressing and tofu and stir to combine.

8. Divide noodles between serving bowls, top with remaining ingredients and garnish with coriander leaves. Serve immediately.

TIPS

To make your own *Tahini*, see pg. 124.

This salad is best eaten on the day it's made.

You can find edamame in the frozen food section of most supermarkets, and the soba noodles in the Asian food aisle.

Varoma **GF** **NF** **EF**

CARROT, FETA AND MINT SALAD

ACTIVE TIME 10 min | TOTAL TIME 40 min | RECIPE MAKES 4 portions

INGREDIENTS

2 garlic cloves

7 sprigs fresh mint, leaves only, torn or cut into pieces

40 g lemon juice

50 g extra virgin olive oil

2 tsp ground cumin

2 tsp paprika

1 tsp sea salt

⅛ tsp ground black pepper

500 g water

700 g Dutch carrots (approx. 3 bunches), peeled and tops trimmed

50–100 g feta cheese, crumbled, for garnishing (see Tips)

USEFUL ITEMS

bowl

large bowl

PREPARATION

1. Place garlic and half of the mint leaves into mixing bowl and chop **3 sec**/**speed 7**. Scrape down sides of mixing bowl with spatula.

2. Add lemon juice, oil, cumin, paprika, salt and pepper and mix **3 sec**/**speed 6**. Transfer into a bowl and set aside.

3. Without cleaning mixing bowl, place water into mixing bowl. Place Varoma into position and weigh carrots into it. Secure Varoma lid and steam **13 min**/**Varoma**/**speed 1**.

4. Stir carrots and cook for a further **2–4 min**/**Varoma**/**speed 1**, or until carrots are cooked to your liking.

5. Transfer carrots into a large bowl. Add reserved dressing and gently stir to combine. Set aside to cool completely (approx. 20 minutes).

6. Serve carrots garnished with crumbled feta and remaining mint leaves.

TIPS

We recommend using Australian or Greek feta in this recipe, as it crumbles easily.

This is a great dish to make ahead for dinner parties or to take to barbecues.

V GF NF

WATERMELON GAZPACHO WITH JALAPEÑO OIL

ACTIVE TIME 20 min | **TOTAL TIME** 1 hr 20 min | **RECIPE MAKES** 6 portions

INGREDIENTS

Jalapeño oil

4 jalapeño chillies, trimmed and deseeded

50 g vegetable oil

1½ tbsp sesame oil

⅛ tsp cumin seeds

½ tsp raw sugar

Watermelon gazpacho

700 g watermelon flesh, deseeded and cut into pieces (4–5 cm)

20 g red onion

40 g red capsicum, deseeded and cut into pieces (4–5 cm)

1½ fresh Lebanese cucumbers, 1 whole cucumber, peeled, deseeded and cut into pieces; ½ cucumber cut into small dice, for garnishing

1 garlic clove

1 tbsp red wine vinegar

40 g olive oil

2 sprigs fresh mint, leaves only

2 sprigs fresh flat-leaf parsley, leaves only

2 sprigs fresh basil, leaves only, plus smaller leaves, for garnishing

10 ice cubes

1 pinch sea salt, to taste

1 pinch ground black pepper, to taste

USEFUL ITEMS

jug

sealable bottle

bowl

PREPARATION

Jalapeño oil

1. Place jalapeños into mixing bowl and chop **3 sec**/**speed 7**. Scrape down sides of mixing bowl with spatula.

2. Add remaining jalapeño oil ingredients and cook **5 min**/**Varoma**/**speed 1**. Transfer into a jug and set aside to cool. Strain into a sealable bottle and set aside until ready to use. Discard solids. Clean and dry mixing bowl.

Watermelon gazpacho

3. Place watermelon, onion, capsicum, cucumber pieces, garlic, vinegar and oil into mixing bowl and blend **1 min**/**speed 10**.

4. Add mint, parsley, basil, ice cubes, salt and pepper and blend **1 min**/**speed 10**. Transfer into a bowl, cover with plastic wrap and place into refrigerator for a minimum of 1 hour before serving.

5. Drizzle with jalapeño oil and garnish with diced cucumber and extra basil before serving.

TIPS

Store leftover oil in a cool, dark place. Drizzle over bruschetta or poached eggs for a bit of heat. Or make your own salsa and use in place of olive oil and/or chillies.

To make this recipe suitable for a raw food diet, simply omit the jalapeño oil.

Varoma   NF   EF   DF

MISO SOUP

ACTIVE TIME 10 min | **TOTAL TIME** 30 min | **RECIPE MAKES** 4 portions

INGREDIENTS

1600 g water

1 kombu strip (7–10 cm) (optional)

5 dried shiitake mushrooms (approx. 20 g), cut into slices

3 cm piece fresh ginger, peeled and cut into thin slices

1 garlic clove, cut into halves

2 tbsp wakame flakes (see Tips)

100 g carrot, peeled and cut into matchsticks or "spaghetti" (see Tips)

150 g daikon, peeled and cut into matchsticks or "spaghetti" (see Tips)

200 g honey soy tofu, cut into cubes (2 cm) (see Tips)

200 g Asian greens of choice, trimmed and cut into pieces (3 cm)

2 tbsp red miso paste (see Tips)

1 tbsp soy sauce

2 tsp sesame oil

1 tsp sea salt, to taste

2 tbsp sesame seeds, for garnishing

3 sprigs fresh coriander, leaves only, for garnishing

2 spring onions/shallots, cut into thin slices, for garnishing

PREPARATION

1. Place water into mixing bowl. Insert simmering basket and place kombu (optional), shiitake mushrooms, ginger, garlic and wakame into it.

2. Place Varoma dish into position and weigh carrots, daikon and tofu into it. Insert Varoma tray and weigh Asian greens onto it. Secure Varoma lid and steam **8–12 min/Varoma/speed 1**, or until vegetables soften. Set Varoma aside. Remove simmering basket with aid of spatula and set aside.

3. Add miso paste, soy, sesame oil and salt to mixing bowl and cook **2 min/100°C/↺/speed ⌓**.

4. Discard kombu, ginger and garlic. Divide vegetables and tofu between bowls, top with soup and garnish with sesame seeds, coriander and spring onion/shallots. Serve immediately.

TIPS

Some vegetable peelers come with an attachment that allows you to cut your vegetables into spaghetti-like strips. Otherwise, peel and very thinly slice your vegetables into narrow strips by hand.

You can marinate your own tofu using the marinade in *Honey ginger tofu with greens* (see pg. 136). You can also purchase marinated tofu at major supermarkets.

Red miso paste can be found in the Asian food aisle in most supermarkets or in Asian grocers. It's also sold as red soya bean paste. For the nutritional benefits of miso, see the Glossary (pg. 178).

Wakame flakes are sold at Asian grocers. For the nutritional benefits of wakame, see the Glossary (pg. 178).

For extra flavour, season your soup with *Wakame gomasio* (see pg. 136).

This soup is a source of calcium, zinc, iron and protein.

BORSCHT WITH POLISH DUMPLINGS

ACTIVE TIME 55 min | **TOTAL TIME** 1 hr 30 min | **RECIPE MAKES** 8 portions

INGREDIENTS

Porcini mushroom filling

30 g dried porcini mushrooms

250 g water

80 g brown onion, cut into quarters

2 tsp oil

30 g breadcrumbs

¼ tsp sea salt

¼ tsp ground black pepper

2 tsp lemon juice

Dumplings

140–160 g plain flour, plus extra for dusting

1 tbsp olive oil

70 g lukewarm water

Borscht

600–700 g raw beetroot, peeled and cut into quarters

3 garlic cloves

5 dried porcini mushrooms, cut into slices

1400 g water

2 tsp sea salt, to taste

¼ tsp ground black pepper, to taste

2 tbsp raw sugar

2 dried bay leaves

5 allspice berries

2–3 tbsp white vinegar, to taste

2 tbsp dried marjoram

USEFUL ITEMS

bowl

silicone bread mat (ThermoMat)

kitchen towel

large saucepan

thermal serving bowl (ThermoServer) or other large bowl

large bowl

PREPARATION

Porcini mushroom filling

1. Place mushrooms into mixing bowl and chop **3 sec/speed 6**.

2. Add water and cook **18 min/100°C/speed 1**.

3. Add onion and oil and chop **3 sec/speed 5**.

4. Scrape down sides of mixing bowl with spatula and cook **2 min/Varoma/speed 1**.

5. Add breadcrumbs, salt, pepper and lemon juice and mix **30 sec/speed 2**.

6. Transfer mushroom mixture into a bowl and set aside. Clean and dry mixing bowl.

Dumplings

7. Place flour, oil and lukewarm water into mixing bowl and knead **1 min/🌾**. Transfer dough onto a silicone bread mat (ThermoMat) or lightly floured work surface.

8. Cut dough into halves. Roll out each dough portion into a rectangle (3 mm thickness). Cut dough portions into squares (6 × 6 cm).

9. Place 1 teaspoon mushroom filling into centre of each dough square and fold edges together diagonally to form a triangle, sealing edges with your fingertips. Gently pull two corners together to form a dumpling, then pinch ends together to seal. Repeat with remaining filling and squares of dough. Cover with kitchen towel and set aside. Clean and dry mixing bowl.

Borscht

10. Place beetroot, garlic and dried mushrooms into mixing bowl and mix **5 sec/speed 5**.

11. Add water, salt, pepper, sugar, bay leaves and allspice and cook **25 min/90°C/speed 1**. Meanwhile, cook dumplings. Place a large saucepan with water over high heat and bring to the boil. Working in 2–3 batches, add dumplings to saucepan and cook until dumplings float to the surface. Using a slotted spoon, remove dumplings and transfer into a thermal serving bowl (ThermoServer) or other large bowl and cover to keep warm.

12. Add vinegar and marjoram to soup in mixing bowl and mix **10 sec/speed 2**.

13. Strain soup through simmering basket into a large bowl and season to taste. Discard contents of simmering basket. Divide soup between 8 serving bowls, then place dumplings into serving bowls before serving.

TIPS

This traditional Polish recipe was contributed by Grace Mazur, Managing Director of Thermomix in Australia and New Zealand. The Polish dumplings (also called "uszka") are often referred to as "Polish Christmas ears" and are traditionally served in borscht at Christmas Eve.

To make this recipe gluten free, simply omit the dumplings.

Borscht is also traditionally served with *Polish croquettes* (see pg. 71).

GF **NF** **EF**

SPICED LENTIL VEGETABLE SOUP

ACTIVE TIME 20 min | **TOTAL TIME** 1 hr 30 min | **RECIPE MAKES** 6 portions

INGREDIENTS

Basic vegetable stock

90 g brown onion, cut into halves

110 g leek, white part only, cut into quarters

260 g carrots, cut into quarters

130 g sweet potato, cut into pieces (3 cm)

120 g celery stalks, cut into quarters

3 dried shiitake mushrooms, cut into slices

4 sprigs fresh flat-leaf parsley

1 dried bay leaf

2 sprigs fresh thyme, leaves only

1300 g water

1 tsp salt

½ tsp ground black pepper

Spiced lentil soup

1 brown onion (approx. 150 g) cut into halves

2 garlic cloves

1–2 fresh red chillies, deseeded if preferred and cut into halves

2 tbsp olive oil

1 tsp ground cumin

¼ tsp ground cayenne pepper

1 tsp salt

200 g red lentils, rinsed and drained

400 g canned diced tomatoes

120 g red capsicum, deseeded and cut into pieces (1–2 cm)

400 g canned mixed beans, rinsed and drained (approx. 250 g after draining)

60 g kale, leaves only (stalks removed) and torn into pieces

4–5 sprigs fresh flat-leaf parsley, cut into pieces

60 g Greek yoghurt (optional)

USEFUL ITEMS

sealable container

large bowl

PREPARATION

Basic vegetable stock

1. Place onion, leek, carrots, sweet potato, celery, mushrooms and parsley into mixing bowl and chop **6 sec/speed 6**. Scrape down sides of mixing bowl with spatula.

2. Add all remaining stock ingredients and cook **60 min/90°C/↻/speed 1**. Transfer into a sealable container and set aside. Clean and dry mixing bowl.

Spiced lentil soup

3. Place onion, garlic and chilli into mixing bowl and chop **3 sec/speed 7**. Scrape down sides of mixing bowl with spatula.

4. Add oil, cumin, cayenne pepper and salt and cook **5 min/100°C/speed 1**.

5. Add lentils, tomatoes, capsicum and 900 g of the reserved vegetable stock and cook **12 min/100°C/speed 1**.

6. Transfer soup into a large bowl. Add mixed beans, kale and parsley and stir to combine. Set aside for 5 minutes to allow kale to wilt.

7. Transfer into serving bowls and top with Greek yoghurt (optional) to serve.

TIPS

For a clear stock, strain through simmering basket or a fine mesh sieve into a sealable container after cooking in step 2. Discard cooked vegetables.

Leftover stock can be frozen or placed into the refrigerator to use in future recipes.

For extra depth of flavour, sprinkle savoury yeast flakes over your soup. It adds a nutty, cheesy flavour and can provide vitamin B12.

This soup provides iron, vitamin C (to aid iron absorption), calcium and is a source of protein. For extra nutrition (such as iodine), add a 5 cm piece of kombu when adding the vegetables in Step 6.

You can replace the canned mixed beans with dried mixed beans (soaked and cooked) in this recipe (see pg. 179).

To aid with digestion and reduce flatulence from the beans, you may want to add a small amount (just a pinch or two) of asafoetida (see Glossary, pg. 178) during step 3. You can buy asafoetida at Indian food stores, some Asian food stores, health food stores and online.

NF EF

JERUSALEM ARTICHOKE SOUP WITH CHEESE SHARDS

ACTIVE TIME 15 min | **TOTAL TIME** 1 hr 10 min | **RECIPE MAKES** 4 portions

INGREDIENTS

Cheese shards

90 g cheddar cheese, cut into pieces (3–4 cm)

40 g Parmesan cheese, crusts removed and cut into pieces (3-4 cm)

90 g unsalted butter, cut into pieces (3–4 cm)

170 g plain flour, plus extra for dusting

½ tsp paprika, plus extra to sprinkle on top

1–2 pinches cayenne pepper

1 tsp sea salt

1 egg

Jerusalem artichoke soup

1 garlic clove

500 g Jerusalem artichokes, peeled and cut into pieces (3–4 cm)

100 g leek, white part only, cut into pieces (3–4 cm)

300 g parsnip, peeled and cut into pieces (3–4 cm)

50 g unsalted butter

1½ tbsp Vegetable stock paste (see Tips)

900 g water

1 apple, cut into quarters

3 sprigs fresh lemon thyme, leaves only

1 tsp lemon zest, no white pith

2 tsp lemon juice

20 g pouring (whipping) cream (optional)

1–2 tsp ground nutmeg, to taste

1–2 pinches sea salt, to taste

1–2 pinches ground black pepper, to taste

USEFUL ITEMS

baking paper

rolling pin

baking tray (30 × 40 cm)

PREPARATION

Cheese shards

1. Preheat oven to 180°C.

2. Place cheddar cheese and Parmesan cheese into mixing bowl and grate **10 sec/speed 8**.

3. Add remaining cheese shard ingredients and knead **30 sec/ᵏ**.

4. Transfer mixture onto a piece of baking paper (35 × 45 cm) and shape dough into a rectangle. Roll dough into a rectangle (approx. 30 × 40 cm) and cut into shards. Transfer baking paper and shards onto a baking tray (30 × 40 cm), sprinkle with extra paprika and bake for 15 minutes (180°C), or until golden brown. Clean and dry mixing bowl.

Jerusalem artichoke soup

5. Place garlic, artichoke, leek, parsnip and butter into mixing bowl and cook **15 min/Varoma/speed 1**.

6. Add stock paste, water and apple and cook **40 min/100°C/speed 1**, or until artichokes and parsnip are soft.

7. Add lemon thyme, lemon zest, lemon juice, cream (optional) and nutmeg and blend **1 min/speed 1–10, increasing speed gradually from speed 1 to speed 10**. Season to taste with salt and pepper.

8. Serve soup with cheese shards.

TIPS

Please refer to *The Basic Cookbook* or *Everyday Cookbook* for the Vegetable stock paste recipe.

For extra depth of flavour, sprinkle savoury yeast flakes over your soup. It adds a nutty, cheesy flavour and may be a source of vitamin B12.

To make this recipe gluten free, simply omit the cheese shards.

MAIN MEALS

NF

PUMPKIN TART

ACTIVE TIME 30 min | **TOTAL TIME** 2 hr 15 min | **RECIPE MAKES** 8 portions

INGREDIENTS

30 g unsalted butter, plus extra for greasing

130 g carrot, cut into pieces (3–4 cm)

100 g parsnip, cut into pieces (3–4 cm)

70 g cheddar cheese, cut into pieces (3–4 cm)

1–2 pinches sea salt, to taste

40 g wholemeal plain flour

1 tbsp chia seeds

2 tbsp poppy seeds

510 g butternut pumpkin, peeled and cut into pieces (3–4 cm)

120 g red onion, cut into halves

1 fresh red chilli, trimmed and deseeded, if preferred (optional)

20 g extra virgin olive oil

1 tbsp brown sugar

60 g water

20 g red wine vinegar

120 g dry white wine

1 dried bay leaf

1 whole clove

120 g feta cheese, crumbled

1 spring onion/shallot, trimmed and cut into thin slices

30 g Parmesan cheese, crust removed and cut into pieces (3 cm)

2 eggs

150 g pouring (whipping) cream

1 tsp caraway seeds (optional)

USEFUL ITEMS

pie dish (23 cm)

baking tray (30 × 40 cm)

baking paper

PREPARATION

1. Preheat oven to 180°C. Grease a pie dish (23 cm) and set aside. Line a baking tray (30 × 40 cm) with baking paper and set aside.

2. Place butter, carrot, parsnip, cheddar cheese, salt, flour, chia seeds, poppy seeds and 260 g of the pumpkin into mixing bowl and chop **4 sec/speed 7**.

3. Transfer mixture into prepared dish, pressing to cover base and sides. Clean and dry mixing bowl.

4. Place remaining 250 g pumpkin onto baking tray. Place baking tray and prepared pie dish into oven and bake for 30 minutes (180°C). Remove from oven and set aside.

5. Place onion, chilli (optional) and oil into mixing bowl and chop **3 sec/speed 5**.

6. Scrape down sides of mixing bowl with spatula and cook **2 min/100°C/speed ⌀**.

7. Add sugar and water and cook **5 min/100°C/speed ⌀, without measuring cup**.

8. Add vinegar, wine, bay leaf and clove and cook for a further **15 min/100°C/speed ⌀, without measuring cup**.

9. Place feta and roasted pumpkin into baked base and top with onion filling mixture. Carefully remove bay leaf and clove and discard.

10. Without cleaning mixing bowl, place spring onion/shallot and Parmesan cheese into mixing bowl and chop **5 sec/speed 7**. Scrape down sides of mixing bowl with spatula.

11. Add eggs and cream and blend **5 sec/speed 5**.

12. Evenly pour topping over tart. Sprinkle with caraway seeds (optional) and bake for 20–25 minutes (180°C), or until golden brown and set in the middle. Allow to cool to room temperature before serving.

MIXED MUSHROOM CONGEE WITH PICKLED EGGS

ACTIVE TIME 30 min | **TOTAL TIME** 1 day 40 min | **RECIPE MAKES** 6 portions

INGREDIENTS

Pickled eggs

1 cinnamon quill

2 dried bay leaves

2 tbsp yellow mustard seeds

½ tsp ground allspice

3 tsp coriander seeds

3 whole cloves

1 tsp dried tarragon

1½ tsp ground ginger

1 tsp dried chilli flakes

2 tsp raw sugar

1 tsp salt

250 g white vinegar

750 g water

6 eggs

Congee

500 g fresh Asian mushrooms (e.g. oyster and enoki), cut into pieces (3–4 cm) (see Tips)

2 spring onions/shallots, trimmed and cut into thin slices

4 cm piece fresh ginger, peeled

150 g eschalot, cut into halves

2 tbsp Vegetable stock paste (see Tips)

1250 g water

180 g jasmine rice

1 tbsp soy sauce, plus extra to serve

1 tbsp sesame oil, plus extra to serve

1 fresh chilli, cut into thin slices, to serve (optional)

2 sprigs fresh coriander, leaves only, to serve

2 tbsp fried Asian shallots, for garnishing

USEFUL ITEMS

sealable container

bowl

thermal serving bowl (ThermoServer) or other large bowl

6 serving bowls

PREPARATION

Pickled eggs

1. Place cinnamon and bay leaves into mixing bowl and chop **3 sec/speed 9**.

2. Add mustard seeds, allspice, coriander seeds, cloves, tarragon, ginger, chilli, sugar and salt and mix **10 sec/speed 4**.

3. Add vinegar and 250 g of the water and cook **5 min/100°C/speed 1**. Transfer into a sealable container and set aside.

4. Place remaining 500 g water into mixing bowl. Insert simmering basket and place eggs into it. Cook **14 min/Varoma/speed 1**, until hard boiled. Remove simmering basket with aid of spatula and carefully transfer eggs into a bowl of cold water. Once cool enough to handle, peel eggs and set aside. Discard cooking water.

5. Place peeled eggs into reserved pickling liquid (ensuring liquid covers eggs completely). Seal and place into refrigerator overnight.

Congee

6. Place a thermal serving bowl (ThermoServer) or other large bowl onto mixing bowl lid and weigh mushrooms into it. Place spring onions/shallots into bowl and set aside.

7. Place ginger and eschalots into mixing bowl and chop **3 sec/speed 7**. Scrape down sides of mixing bowl with spatula.

8. **Insert butterfly whisk**. Add stock paste, water and rice and cook **20 min/100°C/↻/speed ⌀**. **Remove butterfly whisk**.

9. Carefully transfer mixture into thermal serving bowl (ThermoServer) over mushrooms and spring onions/shallots. Cover and leave to stand for 5 minutes to cook mushrooms.

10. Add soy sauce and sesame oil to thermal serving bowl (ThermoServer) and stir to combine.

11. Cut pickled eggs into halves. Divide congee between 6 serving bowls and top with chilli (optional), coriander, fried Asian shallots and pickled eggs. Serve with extra soy sauce and sesame oil.

TIPS

You can use any type of mushrooms you like in this recipe.

Please refer to *The Basic Cookbook* or *Everyday Cookbook* for the Vegetable stock paste recipe.

To make this recipe suitable for those following a vegan diet, omit pickled eggs (steps 1–5).

Eggs are a good source of protein, omega-3 and vitamin B12.

NF

BROCCOLI MUSTARD PASTIES

ACTIVE TIME 35 min | **TOTAL TIME** 1 hr 55 min | **RECIPE MAKES** 6 portions

INGREDIENTS

Quick puff pastry

300 g unsalted butter, cut into small pieces (1–2 cm) and frozen

300 g plain flour, plus extra for flouring

140 g chilled water

Broccoli mustard pasties

180 g cheddar cheese, cut into pieces (3–4 cm)

150 g mozzarella cheese, cut into pieces (3–4 cm)

80 g brown onion, cut into halves

1 garlic clove

100 g swede, peeled and cut into quarters

20 g olive oil

1 tsp English mustard, plus extra to serve

2 tsp Dijon mustard, plus extra to serve

300 g broccoli, broken into florets

1 pinch salt, to taste

1 egg, lightly beaten

3 tsp poppy seeds

USEFUL ITEMS

silicone bread mat (ThermoMat)

plastic wrap

rolling pin

bowl

2 baking trays (30 × 40 cm)

baking paper

pastry brush

PREPARATION

Quick puff pastry

1. Place all pastry ingredients into mixing bowl and mix **20 sec**/**speed 6**.

2. Transfer dough onto a silicone bread mat (ThermoMat) or floured work surface, then shape into a ball and flatten into a rough square. Wrap pastry in plastic wrap and place into refrigerator for 20 minutes.

3. Unwrap dough and place onto silicone bread mat (ThermoMat) or floured work surface. Using a rolling pin, roll out dough into a long rectangle (approx. 60 × 20 cm). Fold dough into thirds and turn folded dough a quarter turn to the left. Repeat rolling, folding and turning two more times. Wrap dough in plastic wrap and place into refrigerator for 20 minutes. Clean and dry mixing bowl.

Broccoli mustard pasties

4. Place cheeses into mixing bowl and grate **10 sec**/**speed 9**. Transfer into a bowl and set aside.

5. Place onion, garlic, swede and oil into mixing bowl and chop **3 sec**/**speed 7**.

6. Scrape down sides of mixing bowl with spatula, then cook **4 min**/**100°C**/**speed 1**.

7. Add mustards, broccoli and salt and mix **5 sec**/↻/**speed 4.5**.

8. Add reserved grated cheeses and mix **5 sec**/↻/**speed 5**.

9. Preheat oven to 190°C. Line 2 baking trays (30 cm × 40 cm) with baking paper and set aside.

10. Remove dough from refrigerator. Divide dough into 6 equal portions. Roll each portion into a circle (20 cm). Divide broccoli mixture between 6 portions and place mixture into the centre of the pastry. Fold pastry over into a half circle shape to enclose filling, crimping edges with a fork to seal. Transfer pasties onto prepared baking trays and place into refrigerator for 10 minutes.

11. Brush pasties with beaten egg and make a small incision into the top of each one (to release steam). Sprinkle with poppy seeds, then bake for 25–30 minutes (190°C), or until puffed and golden. Serve warm with extra mustard on the side.

TIP

Broccoli provides a source of zinc and calcium.

COURGETTE STRUDEL

ACTIVE TIME 45 min | **TOTAL TIME** 1 hr 20 min | **RECIPE MAKES** 6 portions

INGREDIENTS

Basil oil

100 g extra virgin olive oil

3 sprigs fresh basil, leaves only

40 g lemon juice (approx. 1 lemon)

1 pinch sea salt

1 tsp raw sugar

Dough

¼ lemon, zest only, no white pith

60 g semolina (see Tips)

90 g Italian "00" flour, plus extra for dusting (see Tips)

1 tbsp extra virgin olive oil

1 egg white

40 g water

1 pinch sea salt

Filling

50 g Parmesan cheese, crust removed and cut into pieces (3 cm)

½ lemon, zest only, no white pith

4 sprigs fresh flat-leaf parsley, leaves only

4 sprigs fresh basil, leaves only

2 garlic cloves

300 g courgettes, cut into pieces (3 cm)

1 tbsp oil

150 g ricotta cheese, drained well (see Tips)

1 egg

60 g pine nuts

60 g pumpkin seeds

1 pinch ground nutmeg

¼ tsp sea salt, to taste

¼ tsp ground black pepper, to taste

full cream milk, for brushing

PREPARATION

Basil oil

1. Place a jug onto mixing bowl lid and weigh oil into it. Set aside.

2. Place basil, lemon juice, salt and sugar into mixing bowl and chop **3 sec/speed 7**.

3. Scrape down sides of mixing bowl with spatula and mix **2 min/speed 4**, slowly pouring oil onto mixing bowl lid, letting it trickle into mixing bowl. Do not emulsify by overmixing. Transfer dressing into a sealable storage jar or container and set aside until ready to serve. Clean and dry mixing bowl.

Dough

4. Preheat oven to 180°C. Line a baking tray (30 × 40 cm) with baking paper and set aside.

5. Place lemon zest and semolina into mixing bowl and mill **10–20 sec/speed 9**, or until all lemon zest is milled. Scrape down sides of mixing bowl with spatula.

6. Add "00" flour, oil, egg white, water and salt into mixing bowl and knead **3 min/🌾**. Transfer onto a work surface and shape into a ball. Wrap in plastic wrap and place into refrigerator until ready to use. Clean and dry mixing bowl.

Filling

7. Place Parmesan cheese, lemon zest, parsley and basil into mixing bowl and chop **10 sec/speed 7**. Transfer into a bowl and set aside.

8. Place garlic, courgettes and oil into mixing bowl and chop **3 sec/speed 5**.

9. Scrape down sides of mixing bowl with spatula and cook **3 min/100°C/↺/speed 1**. Transfer mixture into simmering basket and set aside to drain (approx. 5 minutes). Place mixture back into mixing bowl.

10. Add ricotta, egg, pine nuts, pumpkin seeds, nutmeg, salt, pepper and reserved parmesan mixture and mix **10 sec/↺/speed 3**.

11. Place dough onto a silicone bread mat (ThermoMat) or lightly floured work surface and roll out into a rectangle (40 × 30 cm). Spread courgette filling onto dough with aid of spatula. Using long edge of the dough, carefully roll into a log shape to enclose filling.

12. Transfer onto prepared tray, brush with milk and bake for 35 minutes (180°C), or until golden brown.

13. Drizzle with Basil oil before serving.

USEFUL ITEMS

jug

sealable storage jar or container

baking tray (30 × 40 cm)

baking paper

plastic wrap

bowl

silicone bread mat (ThermoMat)

rolling pin

pastry brush

TIPS

"00" flour has a finer grain than commercial plain flours, resulting in light and airy bread. It's available in most supermarkets, as well as specialty food stores.

We recommend using fine semolina in this recipe.

To make your own ricotta, visit the My-Thermomix Recipe Platform (www.my-thermomix.com.au) and register to receive your free Welcome Collection, which includes a recipe for homemade ricotta.

Store basil oil in a cool, dark place. Use leftover oil to dress salads or steamed vegetables, or serve with slices of fresh sourdough bread for dipping.

NF **EF**

MEXICAN STACK

ACTIVE TIME 20 min | **TOTAL TIME** 45 min | **RECIPE MAKES** 8 portions

INGREDIENTS

150 g tasty cheese, cut into pieces (3 cm)

2 spring onions/shallots, trimmed and cut into quarters

3 sprigs fresh flat-leaf parsley, leaves only

4 garlic cloves

1 brown onion (approx. 150 g), cut into halves

1–2 fresh chillies, deseeded if preferred

1 tbsp olive oil

1 red capsicum (approx. 220 g), deseeded and cut into pieces

1 zucchini (approx. 325 g), cut into pieces

200 g fresh corn kernels (see Tips)

400 g canned kidney beans, rinsed and drained (approx. 250 g after draining)

70 g tomato paste

400 g canned tomatoes

2 tsp ground cumin

2 tsp ground coriander

2 tsp ground paprika

2 tsp raw sugar

½–1 tsp sea salt, to taste

½–1 tsp ground black pepper, to taste

6 pieces Lebanese flat bread

sour cream, to serve

USEFUL ITEMS

casserole dish

pizza tray

baking paper

bowl

PREPARATION

1. Preheat oven to 180°C. Line a round casserole dish or a rimmed pizza tray (approx. 30 cm) with baking paper and set aside.

2. Place cheese, spring onions/shallots, parsley and 2 of the garlic cloves into mixing bowl and chop **10 sec/speed 5**. Transfer into a bowl and set aside.

3. Place onion, chilli and remaining garlic cloves into mixing bowl and chop **3 sec/speed 7**. Scrape down sides of mixing bowl with spatula.

4. Add oil and cook **3 min/Varoma/speed 1**.

5. Add capsicum, zucchini and 100 g of the corn kernels and chop **5 sec/speed 7**.

6. Add kidney beans, tomato paste, tomatoes, cumin, coriander, paprika, sugar, salt and pepper and cook **15 min/100°C/speed 1**.

7. Add remaining 100 g corn and combine **5 sec/↺/speed 3**.

8. Place a layer of flatbread onto base of prepared dish and spread 2–3 tablespoons of the corn mixture onto bread, smoothing with spatula. Place another layer of flatbread on top, then spread 2–3 tablespoons of the corn mixture onto bread. Continue layering flatbread and the corn mixture, finishing with a layer of corn mixture on top. Sprinkle with reserved cheese mixture and bake for 14–16 minutes (180°C) until cheese is golden and melted. Serve warm with sour cream.

TIPS

You can use thawed frozen corn kernels instead of fresh corn kernels in this recipe.

If you use a pizza tray, ensure it has a lip around all edges to ensure filling and cheese are contained.

You can replace canned beans with dried beans (soaked and cooked) in this recipe (see pg. 179).

Serve with a garden salad, steamed vegetables or cooked black beans.

This dish is a source of zinc, iron, vitamin C and protein.

To aid with digestion and reduce flatulence caused by the fibre in the beans, you may want to add a small amount (just a pinch or two) of asafoetida (see Glossary, pg. 178) during cooking. You can buy asafoetida at Indian food stores, some Asian food stores, health food stores and online.

VEGETABLE PILAF

INGREDIENTS

400 g basmati rice

150 g acorn squash, trimmed, cut into halves and cut into thin slices (5 mm)

160 g red capsicum, deseeded and cut into pieces (1 cm)

150 g fresh green beans, trimmed and cut into quarters

100 g frozen green peas, thawed

280 g marinated artichoke hearts, drained and cut into halves

10 cm piece fresh ginger, peeled

6 garlic cloves

1 brown onion (approx. 150 g), cut into halves

50 g olive oil

2 dried bay leaves

4 cardamom pods, crushed

1 cinnamon quill

2 pinches saffron threads

1 tsp ground smoked paprika

½ tsp chilli powder, to taste

400 g canned chopped tomatoes

3 sprigs fresh thyme, leaves only

100 g dry white wine

2 tsp salt

1 tsp ground black pepper

1 tbsp Vegetable stock paste (see Tips)

600 g water

40 g slivered almonds, for garnishing

USEFUL ITEMS

round casserole dish (28 cm)

bowl

aluminium foil

PREPARATION

1. Preheat oven to 180°C.

2. Place simmering basket onto mixing bowl lid and weigh rice into it. Rinse rice until water runs clear. Transfer rice into a round casserole dish (28 cm) and set aside.

3. Place a bowl onto mixing bowl lid and weigh squash, capsicum, beans, peas and artichokes into it and set aside.

4. Place ginger, garlic, onion and oil into mixing bowl and chop **3 sec/speed 5**. Scrape down sides of mixing bowl with spatula.

5. Add bay leaves, cardamom, cinnamon, saffron, paprika and chilli powder and cook **3 min/Varoma/↺/speed 1**.

6. Add tomatoes, thyme, wine, salt, pepper, stock paste and water and cook **10 min/100°C/↺/speed 1**.

7. Carefully transfer tomato mixture into casserole dish with rice and stir to combine. Cover with a lid or aluminium foil and bake for 20 minutes (180°C).

8. Remove casserole dish from oven, add reserved vegetables and stir to combine (be sure to scrape rice from edges of casserole dish), ensuring that vegetables are coated in rice mixture. Cover and stand for 15–20 minutes, fluffing rice every 5 minutes to ensure even absorption.

9. Remove bay leaves, cinnamon quill and cardamom pods, if desired. Garnish with silvered almonds before serving.

TIPS

Please refer to *The Basic Cookbook* or *Everyday Cookbook* for the Vegetable stock paste recipe.

This recipe is a source of zinc, calcium, iron and vitamin C.

Varoma

RICOTTA PATTIES WITH CHILLI LIME CORN

ACTIVE TIME 20 min | **TOTAL TIME** 1 hr 20 min | **RECIPE MAKES** 4 portions

INGREDIENTS

Coriander salsa

30 g red onion

4 sprigs fresh coriander, leaves only

4 tomatoes, deseeded and cut into pieces (1 cm)

2 tbsp sweet chilli sauce

1 tbsp apple cider vinegar

1 tsp ground cumin

Ricotta patties

50 g walnuts

50 g pecan nuts

250 g day old bread

1 brown onion (approx. 150 g), cut into halves

1 sprig fresh flat-leaf parsley, leaves only

300 g ricotta cheese, drained

3 eggs

2 pinches sea salt, to taste

2 pinches ground black pepper, to taste

1 pinch cayenne pepper, to taste

¼ tsp mustard powder

2 tsp savoury yeast flakes (see Tips)

Chilli lime corn

2 limes, zest only, no white pith, plus extra lime wedges, to serve

6 sprigs fresh coriander, leaves only

1 fresh red chilli, deseeded if preferred, cut into halves

50 g unsalted butter, softened

1 tsp sea salt

½ tsp freshly ground black pepper

4 sweet corn cobs, husks on

500 g water

olive oil, for frying

PREPARATION

Coriander salsa

1. Place onion and coriander into mixing bowl and chop **3 sec/speed 5**.

2. Add remaining salsa ingredients and combine **10 sec/↺/speed 1**.

3. Transfer into a serving bowl and place into refrigerator until ready to serve. Clean and dry mixing bowl.

Ricotta patties

4. Preheat oven to 190°C. Line a baking tray (30 × 40 cm) with baking paper and set aside.

5. Place walnuts, pecans and bread into mixing bowl and chop **3 sec/speed 7**. Transfer onto baking tray and toast for 5 minutes (190°C). Stir nut mixture and toast for a further 5 minutes (190°C). Set aside to cool.

6. Place onion and parsley into mixing bowl and chop **3 sec/speed 7**. Scrape down sides of mixing bowl with spatula.

7. Add all remaining patty ingredients, including reserved nut mixture, and mix **20 sec/speed 3**.

8. Form mixture into 12 round, flat patties (approx. 7 cm diameter). Set aside to rest while making Chilli lime corn. Clean and dry mixing bowl.

Chilli lime corn

9. Place lime zest into mixing bowl and chop **5 sec/speed 7**. Scrape down sides of mixing bowl with spatula.

10. Add coriander and chilli and chop **5 sec/speed 7**. Scrape down sides of mixing bowl with spatula.

11. Add butter, salt and pepper and mix **5 sec/speed 5**. Transfer into a bowl and set aside.

12. Peel away husks from each corn cob, keeping them connected at the bottom. Remove silky corn fibres. Discard outer layers of husks, retaining at least 3 internal layers (reserving enough husk to fully enclose corn). Spread corn cobs with reserved butter mixture. Wrap each cob in its husk to seal in butter.

Continued on page 108

Continued from page 106

USEFUL ITEMS

serving bowl

baking tray (30 × 40 cm)

baking paper

bowl

frying pan

thermal serving bowl (ThermoServer) or plate

13. Place water into mixing bowl. Place Varoma dish into position and place corn cobs into Varoma dish. Secure Varoma lid and steam **25 min**/**Varoma**/**speed 2**, or until corn is tender.

14. Place a frying pan over medium-high heat and add oil. Add patties to pan and fry in batches for approx. 3 minutes each side until golden brown and cooked through. Transfer patties into a thermal serving bowl (ThermoServer) or onto a large plate and cover to keep warm.

15. Serve patties with salsa and corn.

TIP

Savoury yeast flakes may be a source of vitamin B12. You can buy them at health food stores or online.

Varoma **NF** **EF**

VEGETABLE LASAGNE

ACTIVE TIME 45 min | **TOTAL TIME** 1 hr 35 min | **RECIPE MAKES** 8 portions

INGREDIENTS

Lemon and ricotta

1 lemon, zest only, no white pith

1 garlic clove

30 g lemon juice (approx. 1 lemon)

250 g ricotta cheese (see Tips)

Béchamel sauce

50 g unsalted butter

50 g plain flour

450 g full cream milk

¼ tsp sea salt

¼ tsp ground black pepper

Sauce and vegetable filling

100 g Parmesan cheese, crust removed and cut into pieces (3 cm)

1 brown onion (approx. 150 g), cut into halves

2 garlic cloves

1 fresh red chilli, deseeded if preferred, cut into pieces

40 g olive oil

800 g canned whole tomatoes

100 g red wine

3 sprigs fresh basil, leaves only, torn into pieces

4 sprigs fresh flat-leaf parsley, leaves only, torn into pieces

2 tbsp dried oregano

1 tsp sea salt

1 tsp ground black pepper

300 g sweet potato, peeled and cut into slices (1 cm)

1 eggplant (approx. 260 g), cut into slices (1 cm)

1 zucchini (approx. 260 g), cut into slices (1 cm)

250 g button mushrooms, cut into slices

3 kale leaves, stalks removed and leaves torn into pieces (optional)

butter, for greasing

500 g fresh lasagne sheets

salad greens, to serve

PREPARATION

Lemon and ricotta

1. Place lemon zest and garlic into mixing bowl and grate **20 sec/speed 7**. Scrape down sides of mixing bowl with spatula.

2. Add lemon juice and ricotta and mix **10 sec/speed 3**. Transfer into a bowl and set aside.

Béchamel sauce

3. Without cleaning mixing bowl, place all béchamel sauce ingredients into mixing bowl and cook **7 min/90°C/speed 4**. Transfer into a jug, cover and set aside. Clean and dry mixing bowl.

Sauce and vegetable filling

4. Place Parmesan cheese into mixing bowl and grate **10 sec/speed 10**. Transfer into a bowl and set aside. Clean and dry mixing bowl.

5. Place onion, garlic and chilli into mixing bowl and chop **3 sec/speed 7**. Scrape down sides of mixing bowl with spatula.

6. Add oil and cook **3 min/100°C/speed 1**.

7. Add tomatoes, wine, basil, parsley, oregano, salt and pepper. Place Varoma dish into position and weigh sweet potato and eggplant into it. Insert Varoma tray and weigh zucchini and mushrooms onto it. Secure Varoma lid and steam **15 min/Varoma/speed 1**. Set Varoma aside.

8. Add kale (optional) into mixing bowl, place Varoma back into position, secure Varoma lid and cook **2 min/Varoma/speed 2**.

Continued on page 110

Continued from page 109

USEFUL ITEMS

bowl

jug

casserole dish (40 × 25 × 6 cm)

Assembly

9. Preheat oven to 180°C. Lightly grease a casserole dish (40 × 25 × 6 cm).

10. Cover base of casserole dish with a thin layer of tomato sauce (approx. 3-4 tablespoons). Place a layer of lasagne sheets over sauce, cover with all of the eggplant, one-third of the reserved béchamel sauce and one-third of the tomato sauce.

11. Cover sauce with another layer of lasagne sheets. Top with all of the zucchini, one-third of the tomato sauce and half of the lemon ricotta.

12. Cover ricotta with another layer of lasagne sheets. Top with all of the sweet potato and one-third of the béchamel sauce.

13. Cover béchamel with another layer of lasagne sheets. Top with all of the mushrooms and remaining béchamel sauce. Cover with remaining lasagne sheets and remaining tomato sauce. Top with remaining lemon ricotta, then sprinkle with reserved Parmesan cheese. Bake for 30-35 minutes (180°C), or until cheese is golden. Serve immediately with a green salad.

TIPS

This recipe provides a number of nutrients, including iron, calcium, vitamin B12, vitamin C and protein.

To make your own ricotta, visit the My-Thermomix Recipe Platform (www.my-thermomix.com.au) and register to receive your free Welcome Collection, which includes a recipe for homemade ricotta.

BUCKWHEAT AND MUSHROOM QUICHE

ACTIVE TIME 10 min | **TOTAL TIME** 1 day 5 hr 20 min | **RECIPE MAKES** 8 portions

INGREDIENTS

Base

80 g buckwheat, soaked overnight

1–2 garlic cloves, to taste (see Tips)

70 g red onion

6 sprigs fresh flat-leaf parsley, leaves only

90 g carrot, cut into quarters

1 celery stalk, cut into quarters

50 g walnuts

1 tbsp ground coriander

1 tbsp Bragg's® liquid aminos (see Tips)

1 pinch sea salt

Filling

3 fresh Portobello mushrooms, cut into slices

2 tbsp tamari

3 tbsp extra virgin olive oil

1–2 garlic cloves, to taste (see Tips)

100 g raw cashew nuts

80 g pine nuts

30 g lemon juice (approx. 1 lemon)

1 pinch sea salt

50 g fresh baby spinach leaves

2 sprigs fresh basil, leaves only

100 g rocket, to serve

USEFUL ITEMS

ceramic pie dish (25 cm)

bowl

PREPARATION

Base

1. Place soaked buckwheat into simmering basket and rinse until water runs clear. Set aside to drain.

2. Place garlic, onion and parsley into mixing bowl and chop **5 sec/speed 5**. Scrape down sides of mixing bowl with spatula.

3. Add all remaining base ingredients, including drained buckwheat, and blend **20 sec/speed 6**.

4. Scrape down sides of mixing bowl with spatula and blend **20 sec/speed 5**.

5. Press mixture in ceramic pie dish (25 cm) using wet hands. Place into dehydrator (40°C) for 3–4 hours or until dry and base retains shape. Turn off dehydrator and leave base in dehydrator until ready to fill (no more than 6 hours). Clean and dry mixing bowl.

Filling

6. Place mushrooms, tamari and 2 tablespoons of the oil into a bowl and stir to combine, then set aside.

7. Place garlic into mixing bowl and chop **3 sec/speed 6**. Transfer into bowl with mushroom mixture, stir to combine and set aside.

8. Place cashews and 40 g of the pine nuts into mixing bowl and mill **7 sec/speed 8**. Scrape down sides of mixing bowl with spatula.

9. Add lemon juice, salt and remaining 1 tablespoon oil and blend **10 sec/speed 6** until smooth. Scrape down sides of mixing bowl with spatula. Adjust seasoning as needed.

10. Add spinach, basil and mushroom mixture and combine **10 sec/↺/speed 3**. Transfer mixture into a bowl and place into refrigerator until cold (approx. 1 hour).

11. Transfer mushroom filling into base and spread evenly using the spatula. Garnish with remaining 40 g pine nuts and rocket just before serving.

TIPS

As this dish is raw, adjust the amount of garlic used according to your preference.

This dish provides iron and zinc, and is a source of protein.

You can buy Bragg's® liquid aminos (see Glossary, pg. 178) at health food stores or online.

SEMOLINA GNOCCHI WITH ASPARAGUS

ACTIVE TIME 20 min | **TOTAL TIME** 1 hr 15 min | **RECIPE MAKES** 6 portions

INGREDIENTS

Semolina gnocchi

20 g unsalted butter, plus extra for greasing

80 g Parmesan cheese, crust removed and cut into pieces (3 cm)

1000 g full cream milk

½ tsp sea salt

1–2 pinches ground nutmeg

2 egg yolks

290 g semolina (see Tips)

Walnut and basil pesto

40 g fresh basil leaves (approx. 1 bunch) (see Tips)

100 g walnuts

50 g Parmesan cheese, crust removed and cut into pieces (2 cm)

½ garlic clove

130 g olive oil

1 pinch salt, to taste

1 pinch ground black pepper, to taste

Vegetable topping

2 garlic cloves

2 tsp avocado oil, plus extra for drizzling (see Tips)

2 tsp balsamic glaze, plus extra for drizzling

2 tbsp water

200 g Brussels sprouts, trimmed and cut into halves

200 g asparagus, cut into pieces (3 cm)

2 pinch sea salt, to taste

2 pinches ground black pepper, to taste

USEFUL ITEMS

casserole dish (33 × 23 × 5 cm)

bowl

silicone bread mat (ThermoMat)

baking paper

sealable container

serving bowls

PREPARATION

Semolina gnocchi

1. Preheat oven to 200°C. Grease a casserole dish (33 × 23 × 5 cm) and set aside.

2. Place Parmesan cheese into mixing bowl and grate **10 sec/speed 9**. Transfer into a bowl and set aside.

3. Place milk, salt, nutmeg and butter into mixing bowl and cook **8 min/100°C/speed 2**.

4. Add egg yolks, 250 g of the semolina and 40 g of the grated cheese and cook **4 min/90°C/speed 4**.

5. Scrape down sides of mixing bowl with spatula and cook **1–2 min/90°C/speed 4**, or until semolina is cooked.

6. Spread 20 g of the uncooked semolina in a thin layer on a silicone bread mat (ThermoMat) or piece of baking paper (approx 60 × 40 cm). Carefully pour hot semolina mixture on top of the uncooked semolina. Sprinkle remaining 20 g uncooked semolina over hot mixture. Allow to cool (approx. 10 minutes). Clean and dry mixing bowl.

7. Cut gnocchi into squares (4 cm) and transfer into prepared casserole dish. Sprinkle with remaining Parmesan and bake for 15–20 minutes (200°C) until golden and Parmesan has melted.

Walnut and basil pesto

8. Place all pesto ingredients into mixing bowl and blend **10 sec/speed 6**, or until smooth. Transfer into a sealable container and set aside. Clean and dry mixing bowl.

Vegetable topping

9. Place garlic into mixing bowl and chop **3 sec/speed 7**. Scrape down sides of mixing bowl with spatula.

10. Add avocado oil, balsamic glaze and water and cook **1 min/100°C/speed 1**.

11. Add Brussels sprouts, asparagus, salt and pepper and cook **4–6 min/100°C/⟲/speed ⋓**, or until cooked to your preference.

12. Divide gnocchi between serving bowls and top with a few spoonfuls of pesto. Add Brussels sprouts and asparagus, then drizzle with extra avocado oil and balsamic glaze before serving.

Continued on page 116

Continued from page 114

TIPS

We used fine semolina in this recipe. Coarse semolina will also work, although you may need to increase the cooking time in step 4 to ensure that it is cooked through.

When adding basil leaves into the mixing bowl, be sure to add them in handfuls, as individual leaves may not register on the scales.

Top pesto with a layer of olive oil, then store in the refrigerator. Ensure that pesto is always covered with a layer of oil to ensure it doesn't dry out.

Make the pesto and vegetable topping while the gnocchi are baking.

If you don't have avocado oil, use grapeseed oil, or any other light-flavoured oil.

This recipe provides both calcium and vitamin B12, and is a good source of protein.

VARIATION

If you are in a hurry, sprinkle 20 g uncooked semolina into the greased casserole dish and pour hot semolina mixture straight into the dish. Sprinkle with remaining 20 g uncooked semolina and grated Parmesan and bake as per recipe.

THREE BEAN SHEPHERD'S PIE

ACTIVE TIME 30 min | **TOTAL TIME** 1 day 2 hr | **RECIPE MAKES** 6 portions

INGREDIENTS

Vegetable filling

80 g dried chickpeas

80 g dried borlotti beans

80 g dried kidney beans

1130 g water

20 g dried shiitake mushrooms, cut into slices

2 garlic cloves

⅛ tsp asafoetida powder (optional) (see Tips)

1 brown onion (approx. 150 g), cut into halves

20 g unsalted butter

6 sprigs fresh flat-leaf parsley, leaves only

170 g tomatoes, cut into halves

200 g zucchini, trimmed and cut into quarters

70 g celery stalks, cut into quarters

150 g potatoes, peeled and cut into pieces (2 cm)

120 g carrot, peeled and cut into pieces (2 cm)

2 tbsp Vegetable stock paste (see Tips)

2 tsp dried thyme

1 tsp salt

1 tsp ground black pepper

60 g red wine

50 g tomato paste

100 g field mushrooms, cut into slices (5 mm)

Sweet potato topping

50 g Parmesan cheese, crust removed and cut into pieces (3 cm)

250 g full cream milk

⅛ tsp sea salt, to taste

⅛ tsp ground black pepper, to taste

1000 g sweet potato, peeled and cut into pieces (3–4 cm)

30 g unsalted butter

PREPARATION

1. Place all dried beans and 1000 g of the water into a bowl, then cover and soak overnight.

Vegetable filling

2. Place shiitake mushrooms and remaining 130 g water into a bowl and set aside.

3. Drain beans and set aside.

4. Place garlic, asafoetida (optional), onion, butter, parsley, tomato, zucchini and celery into mixing bowl and chop **3 sec/speed 7**.

5. Scrape down sides of mixing bowl with spatula and cook **5 min/100°C/speed 1**.

6. Add potato, carrots, stock paste, thyme, salt, pepper, wine, shiitake mushrooms with soaking liquid and drained beans. Stir mixture with spatula and cook **12 min/100°C/↻/speed ◁**.

7. Add tomato paste and field mushrooms, stir with spatula and cook **15–18 min/100°C/↻/speed ◁**, placing simmering basket instead of measuring cup onto mixing bowl lid, until beans are soft.

8. Divide filling between 6 ramekins or other heat-resistant dishes (300 ml) and set aside.

9. Preheat oven to 180°C. Clean and dry mixing bowl.

Sweet potato topping

10. Place Parmesan into mixing bowl and grate **10 sec/speed 9**. Transfer into a small bowl and set aside. Clean and dry mixing bowl.

11. Place milk, salt, pepper and sweet potato into mixing bowl and cook **25 min/90°C/speed 1**.

12. Chop **30 sec/speed 4**, then scrape down sides of mixing bowl with spatula.

13. **Insert butterfly whisk**. Add butter and three-quarters of the reserved Parmesan and mash **20 sec/speed 4**. Season to taste. **Remove butterfly whisk**.

14. Spoon mash over vegetable filling in ramekins and spread using spatula. Sprinkle with remaining Parmesan and bake for 20–25 minutes (180°C), or until top is lightly browned. Serve immediately.

Continued on page 118

Continued from page 117

USEFUL ITEMS

bowl

plastic wrap

6 ramekins or other heat-resistant dishes (300 ml)

small bowl

TIPS

You can replace dried beans with canned beans in this recipe, however be sure to rinse and drain the canned beans prior to cooking to remove any excess sodium (see pg. 179).

Please refer to *The Basic Cookbook* or *Everyday Cookbook* for the Vegetable stock paste recipe.

You can make the vegetable filling up to 2 days in advance and store in the refrigerator (through Step 8). When ready, make the sweet potato topping and proceed as per recipe. You can also freeze the filling for up to 1 month. Defrost filling in the refrigerator overnight, then make sweet potato topping and proceed as per recipe.

This recipe is a source of zinc, iron, vitamin C (to aid iron absorption) and protein.

To aid with digestion and reduce flatulence caused by the fibre in the beans, you may want to add a small amount (just a pinch or two) of asafoetida (see Glossary, pg. 178) during cooking. You can buy asafoetida at Indian food stores, some Asian food stores, health food stores and online.

Varoma **EF**

MACARONI CHEESE WITH A CRUNCHY TOPPING

ACTIVE TIME 20 min | **TOTAL TIME** 1 hr 10 min | **RECIPE MAKES** 6 portions

INGREDIENTS

Nut topping

1 lemon, zest only, no white pith

100 g Parmesan cheese, crust removed and cut into pieces (3 cm)

2 slices bread (approx. 70 g), torn into pieces

1 sprig fresh rosemary, leaves only

50 g raw almonds

70 g unsalted butter

20 g pepita seeds (optional)

20 g sunflower seeds (optional)

1 pinch sea salt

1 pinch ground black pepper

Macaroni cheese

60 g unsalted butter, plus extra for greasing

90 g Gruyère cheese, cut into pieces (3 cm)

50 g Parmesan cheese, crust removed and cut into pieces (3 cm)

60 g leek, white part only, cut into pieces

200 g cauliflower, cut into florets

150 g sweet potato, peeled and cut into cubes (2 cm)

1200 g water

300 g macaroni pasta

50 g plain flour

500 g full cream milk

¼–1 tsp ground nutmeg, to taste

1 tsp paprika, to taste

2 tsp Dijon mustard

1 pinch sea salt, to taste

1 pinch ground black pepper, to taste

USEFUL ITEMS

bowl

baking dish (22 × 30 cm)

large bowl

PREPARATION

Nut topping

1. Place lemon zest and Parmesan cheese into mixing bowl and grate **10 sec/speed 7**.

2. Add bread, rosemary and almonds and chop **10 sec/speed 7**. Transfer into a bowl and set aside.

3. Place butter into mixing bowl and melt **2 min/50ºC/speed 1**.

4. Add reserved bread mixture and remaining nut topping ingredients and combine **10 sec/↻/speed 2**. Transfer into a bowl and set aside. Clean and dry mixing bowl.

Macaroni cheese

5. Preheat oven to 200ºC. Grease a baking dish (22 × 30 cm) and set aside.

6. Place cheeses into mixing bowl and grate **5 sec/speed 9**. Transfer into a bowl and set aside.

7. Place Varoma into position, then weigh leeks, cauliflower and sweet potato into Varoma and set aside.

8. Place water into mixing bowl and bring to the boil **10 min/Varoma/speed 1**.

9. Add macaroni to mixing bowl and place Varoma into position. Secure Varoma lid and cook **10 min/Varoma/↻/speed 1**. Set Varoma aside. Drain pasta and transfer into a large bowl.

10. Place cooked vegetables and 30 g of the butter into mixing bowl and purée **10 sec/speed 8**. Transfer into bowl with pasta and stir to combine. Clean and dry mixing bowl.

11. Place flour, milk and remaining 30 g butter into mixing bowl and cook **6 min/90ºC/speed 4**.

12. Add nutmeg, paprika, mustard, salt, pepper and reserved cheeses and cook **2 min/90ºC/speed 2**. Transfer into bowl with pasta and stir to combine.

13. Pour pasta mixture into prepared baking dish and top with reserved nut mixture. Bake for 15–20 minutes (200ºC), or until bubbling and golden brown. Serve immediately.

TIP

This recipe contains calcium and B vitamins.

GF **NF** **EF**

ROASTED PUMPKIN AND QUINOA RISOTTO

ACTIVE TIME 10 min | **TOTAL TIME** 40 min | **RECIPE MAKES** 4 portions

INGREDIENTS

500 g butternut pumpkin, cut into cubes (3 cm)

1 fresh chilli, deseeded and cut into thin slices (optional), plus extra to serve

1–2 pinches salt, plus extra to season

1–2 pinches ground black pepper, plus extra to season

olive oil, for drizzling

3 sprigs fresh rosemary, leaves only

3 sprigs fresh thyme, leaves only

60 g Parmesan cheese, crust removed and cut into pieces (3 cm), plus extra to serve

1 brown onion (approx. 150 g), cut into quarters

80 g unsalted butter, cut into pieces

550 g water

2 tsp Vegetable stock paste (see Tips)

250 g white quinoa, rinsed and drained

80 g pouring (whipping) cream

2 sprigs fresh basil, leaves only, torn into pieces

USEFUL ITEMS

baking tray (30 × 40 cm)

baking paper

bowl

PREPARATION

1. Preheat oven to 200°C. Line a baking tray (30 × 40 cm) with baking paper. Place pumpkin and chilli (optional) onto tray, season with salt and pepper and drizzle with oil. Bake for 15–20 minutes (200°C), or until golden brown. Meanwhile, proceed with recipe.

2. Place rosemary, thyme and Parmesan into mixing bowl and grate **10 sec/speed 9**. Transfer into a bowl and set aside. Clean and dry mixing bowl.

3. Place onion and butter into mixing bowl and chop **3 sec/speed 5**.

4. Scrape down sides of mixing bowl with spatula and sauté **3 min/Varoma/speed 1**.

5. Add water, stock paste and quinoa and cook **15–17 min/100°C/◔/speed 1**, or until quinoa is cooked.

6. Add cream and reserved Parmesan mixture and combine **1 min/◔/speed 3.5**. Season to taste.

7. Divide risotto between 4 serving bowls, top with pumpkin and chilli (optional) and garnish with torn basil and extra Parmesan. Serve immediately.

TIPS

Please refer to *The Basic Cookbook* or *Everyday Cookbook* for the Vegetable stock paste recipe.

Quinoa is one of the few plant foods that is considered to be a complete protein, and ideal for those following a vegetarian diet.

NF

LENTIL AND CHICKPEA BURGER WITH TAHINI DRESSING

ACTIVE TIME 45 min | **TOTAL TIME** 1 hr 30 min | **RECIPE MAKES** 8 portions

INGREDIENTS

Tahini

200 g sesame seeds

50 g grapeseed oil

1 pinch sea salt

Tahini dressing

2 tbsp lemon juice

1 tsp onion salt

1 tsp honey

50 g soy milk

1 pinch granulated garlic

Lentil and chickpea burgers

100 g cheddar cheese, cut into pieces (3–4 cm)

150 g day-old bread, torn into pieces

4 sprigs fresh flat-leaf parsley, leaves only

1 red onion (approx. 80 g), cut into halves

1 garlic clove

1 tbsp dried oregano

1 tsp mustard powder

1–2 pinches cayenne pepper

1 tbsp olive oil, plus extra for frying

400 g canned lentils, rinsed and drained (approx. 250 g drained)

400 g canned chickpeas, rinsed and drained (approx. 250 g drained)

1 egg

Assembly

8 bread rolls

1 avocado, flesh only

200 g Brie cheese, cut into thin slices (optional)

1–2 ripe Roma tomatoes, cut into slices

4 leaves cos lettuce, torn into pieces

PREPARATION

Tahini

1. Place sesame seeds into mixing bowl and roast **8 min/100°C/speed 1**. Set aside in mixing bowl to cool (approx. 10 minutes).

2. Mill **20 sec/speed 10**. Scrape down sides of mixing bowl with spatula.

3. Add oil and salt and purée **10 sec/speed 9**.

4. Scrape down sides of mixing bowl with spatula and mix **10 sec/speed 9**. Transfer into a sealable jar or container and place into refrigerator until ready to use.

Tahini dressing

5. Place lemon juice and 3 tablespoons of the reserved tahini into mixing bowl and mix **3 sec/speed 4**.

6. Add all remaining dressing ingredients and mix **5 sec/speed 4**.

7. Scrape down sides of mixing bowl with spatula and mix **5 sec/speed 4**. Transfer into a sealable container and place into refrigerator until ready to serve. Clean and dry mixing bowl.

Lentil and chickpea burgers

8. Place cheddar cheese, bread and parsley into mixing bowl and grate **10 sec/speed 5**. Transfer into a bowl and set aside.

9. Place onion, garlic, oregano, mustard powder, cayenne and oil into mixing bowl and chop **3 sec/speed 5**.

10. Scrape down sides of mixing bowl with spatula and cook **3 min/100°C/speed 1**.

11. Add lentils and chickpeas and chop **10 sec/speed 4**. Scrape down sides of mixing bowl with spatula.

12. Add egg, reserved cheese mixture and 2 tablespoons of the reserved tahini and combine **30 sec/↺/speed 2**, with aid of spatula. Form into 8 patties (approx. 120 g each), transfer onto a plate and place into refrigerator for 15 minutes.

13. Place a frying pan over medium heat and add a little of the extra oil. Cook patties for 3–5 minutes on each side, or until golden brown and cooked to your liking.

Assembly

14. Cut bread rolls into halves horizontally and toast. Spread rolls with avocado. Place a slice each of Brie (optional) and tomato on bottom halves of rolls. Top with a patty, a dollop of Tahini dressing and lettuce. Serve immediately.

sealable storage jar or container

sealable container

bowl

serving plate

frying pan

TIPS

Unhulled sesame seeds can also be used to make tahini; they provide more nutrients, but will result in a darker, slightly bitter tahini.

This recipe includes a range of nutrients, including iron, zinc, calcium, vitamin B12 and protein.

You can store Tahini in the refrigerator for 2-3 weeks.

You can store Tahini dressing in the refrigerator for up to 1 week. Use leftover dressing on green salads, couscous salads, or as a dip for veggie sticks.

You can replace canned chickpeas with dried chickpeas (soaked and cooked) in this recipe (see pg. 179).

To aid with digestion and reduce flatulence caused by the fibre in the legumes, you may want to add a small amount (just a pinch or two) of asafoetida (see Glossary, pg. 178) during step 9. You can buy asafoetida at Indian food stores, some Asian food stores, health food stores and online.

Varoma

HARVEST NUT ROAST WITH GRAVY

ACTIVE TIME 25 min | **TOTAL TIME** 1 hr 30 min | **RECIPE MAKES** 6 portions

INGREDIENTS

Harvest nut roast

2 tbsp olive oil, plus extra for greasing

100 g sourdough bread, torn into pieces

75 g roasted unsalted cashews

80 g raw almonds

1 sprig fresh rosemary, leaves only

2 tsp dried thyme

2 tsp dried oregano

3 sprigs fresh flat-leaf parsley, leaves only

80 g full cream milk

500 g water

250 g parsnip, peeled and cut into pieces (1–2 cm)

250 g carrot, peeled and cut into pieces (1–2 cm)

250 g potato, peeled and cut into pieces (1–2 cm)

250 g turnip, peeled and cut into pieces (1–2 cm)

¼ tsp sea salt, to taste

¼ tsp ground black pepper, to taste

1 brown onion (approx. 150 g), cut into halves

3 tsp Moroccan spice

½ tsp ground chilli

400 g canned cannellini beans, rinsed and drained (approx. 250 g after draining)

2 eggs

80 g walnuts, cut into pieces

Traditional style gravy

80 g red onion, cut into halves

3 garlic cloves

2 tbsp olive oil

150 g cashews

2 tsp red wine vinegar

1 tbsp plain flour

2 tbsp soy sauce

1 tbsp savoury yeast flakes (see Tips)

300 g water

PREPARATION

Harvest nut roast

1. Preheat oven to 180°C. Grease and line a loaf tin (25 × 9 × 11 cm) and set aside.

2. Place bread, cashews, almonds and herbs into mixing bowl and chop **5 sec/speed 7**. Scrape down sides of mixing bowl with spatula.

3. Add milk and combine **5 sec/↩/speed 3**. Transfer into a bowl and set aside. Clean and dry mixing bowl.

4. Place water into mixing bowl. Place Varoma dish into position and weigh parsnip, carrot, potato and turnip into it. Season with salt and pepper. Transfer half of the vegetables onto Varoma tray, place tray into position, secure Varoma lid and steam **10 min/Varoma/speed 1**.

5. Stir vegetables, secure Varoma lid and cook **5 min/Varoma/speed 1**. Transfer vegetables into a large bowl and set aside. Discard water.

6. Place onion into mixing bowl and chop **3 sec/speed 7**. Scrape down sides of mixing bowl with spatula.

7. Add oil, Moroccan spice and ground chilli and cook **1 min/Varoma/speed 1**.

8. Add cannellini beans, eggs, walnuts and reserved bread mixture and combine **10 sec/↩/speed 3**. Transfer into bowl with vegetables and stir to combine.

9. Transfer mixture into loaf tin and bake for 35–40 minutes (180°C) until golden brown. Set aside to cool for 10 minutes. Clean and dry mixing bowl.

Traditional style gravy

10. Place onion and garlic into mixing bowl and chop **3 sec/speed 7**. Scrape down sides of mixing bowl with spatula.

11. Add oil and cook **3 min/Varoma/speed 1**.

12. Add cashews and mill **10 sec/speed 8**.

13. Add all remaining gravy ingredients and blend **2 min/speed 8**, until smooth and creamy.

14. Scrape down sides of mixing bowl with spatula and cook **7–10 min/100°C/speed 1**, or until slightly thickened.

15. Serve nut roast with gravy.

USEFUL ITEMS

loaf tin (25 x 9 x 11 cm)

baking paper

bowl

large bowl

TIPS

You can buy savoury yeast flakes (which can be a source of vitamin B12) at health food stores or online.

You can replace canned beans with dried beans (soaked and cooked) in this recipe (see pg. 179).

Serve this roast with steamed vegetables such as broccolini, snap peas or green beans. You can steam them over the gravy, depending on the size of your vegetables and desired texture of your gravy.

To aid with digestion and reduce flatulence caused by the fibre in the beans, you may want to add a small amount (just a pinch or two) of asafoetida (see Glossary, pg. 178) during step 6. You can buy asafoetida at Indian food stores, some Asian food stores, health food stores and online.

Varoma **NF** **EF**

AUTUMN VEGETABLE GRATIN

ACTIVE TIME 15 min | **TOTAL TIME** 1 hr | **RECIPE MAKES** 6 portions

INGREDIENTS

olive oil, for greasing

50 g Parmesan cheese, crust removed and cut into pieces (3 cm)

1 lemon, zest only, no white pith

2 garlic cloves

1 tbsp savoury yeast flakes (see Tips)

100 g day-old bread, torn into pieces

500 g water

1 swede (approx. 160 g), peeled and cut into thin slices (5 mm)

1 potato (approx. 100 g), peeled and cut into thin slices (5 mm)

2 fennel bulbs, trimmed, core removed and cut into slices (5 mm)

1 zucchini, cut into thin slices (5 mm)

1 red onion, cut into thin slices (5 mm)

2–3 fresh tomatoes, cut into thin slices (5 mm)

1 tsp dried oregano

1 tsp dried thyme

⅛ tsp sea salt, to taste

⅛ tsp ground black pepper, to taste

USEFUL ITEMS

casserole dish (28 × 21 cm)

bowl

PREPARATION

1. Preheat oven to 190°C. Grease an ovenproof casserole dish (28 × 21 cm) and set aside.

2. Place Parmesan cheese and lemon zest into mixing bowl and mill **10 sec/speed 8**.

3. Add garlic, savoury yeast flakes and bread and chop **3 sec/speed 7**. Transfer bread mixture into a bowl and set aside.

4. Place water into mixing bowl. Place Varoma dish into position and place swede, potato and fennel into it. Insert Varoma tray and place zucchini and onion onto it. Secure Varoma lid and cook **15–20 min/Varoma/speed 1**, or until tender.

5. Layer cooked vegetables into prepared casserole dish. Top with tomato slices and herbs, then season with salt and pepper. Cover with bread mixture and bake for 20–25 minutes (190°C), or until top is golden and crisp. Serve warm.

TIPS

To make this recipe gluten free, replace bread with gluten free bread.

You can buy savoury yeast flakes (which can be a source of vitamin B12) at health food stores and online.

CHEESE AND SPRING ONION GALETTE

ACTIVE TIME 25 min | **TOTAL TIME** 1 hr 15 min | **RECIPE MAKES** 6 portions

INGREDIENTS

Pastry

70 g unsalted butter, chilled and cut into pieces (3-4 cm)

120 g self-raising flour, plus extra for dusting

2 pinches sea salt

1 egg yolk

30 g chilled water

Filling

200 g cheddar cheese, cut into pieces (3 cm)

40 g unsalted butter

140 g spring onion/shallot, trimmed, white portion cut into halves and green portion cut into thin slices

100 g flaked almonds

1 tbsp wholegrain mustard

2 egg yolks

1 egg

1 tsp dried marjoram

2 tbsp full cream milk

Creamy tofu dressing

200 g extra virgin olive oil

3 garlic cloves

150 g silken tofu

1 tbsp seeded mustard

60 g balsamic vinegar

2 tbsp miso paste (see Tips)

USEFUL ITEMS

baking tray (30 × 40 cm)

plastic wrap

baking paper

rolling pin

bowl

pastry brush

jug

PREPARATION

Pastry

1. Preheat oven to 170ºC. Set aside a baking tray (30 × 40 cm).

2. Place butter, flour and salt into mixing bowl and mix **10 sec/speed 6**, or until mixture resembles breadcrumbs.

3. Add egg yolk and water and blend **5 sec/speed 5**. Transfer onto a clean work surface, shape into a ball and wrap in plastic wrap. Place into refrigerator for 15 minutes.

4. Transfer dough onto a lightly floured piece of baking paper (30 × 40 cm) and roll dough into a circle (30 cm diameter). Transfer pastry with baking paper onto baking tray and set aside. Do not clean mixing bowl.

Filling

5. Place cheese into mixing bowl and grate **5 sec/speed 8**. Transfer into a bowl and set aside. Clean and dry mixing bowl.

6. Place butter and white portion of the spring onions/shallots into mixing bowl and chop **3 sec/speed 5**.

7. Scrape down sides of mixing bowl with spatula and cook **3 min/100ºC/speed 1**.

8. Add all remaining filling ingredients, except milk, including reserved cheese and combine **5 sec/⟲/speed 3**.

9. Spread mixture onto pastry, leaving a 5 cm border on all sides. Fold over pastry border, pleating pastry as you fold to create a crust. Brush top of pastry with milk and bake for 25–30 minutes (170ºC), or until pastry is puffed and golden. Meanwhile, make creamy tofu dressing while galette bakes. Clean and dry mixing bowl.

Creamy tofu dressing

10. Place a jug onto mixing bowl lid and weigh oil into it. Set aside.

11. Place garlic into mixing bowl and chop **3 sec/speed 7**. Scrape down sides of mixing bowl with spatula.

12. Add all remaining dressing ingredients, except oil, and mix **3 sec/speed 4**. Scrape down sides of mixing bowl with spatula.

13. **Insert butterfly whisk**. Mix **2 min/speed 4**, slowly pouring oil onto mixing bowl lid, letting it trickle into mixing bowl.

14. Allow to cool for 5–10 minutes before serving with galette.

TIPS

You can use any variety/colour of miso paste in this recipe. For the nutritional benefits of miso, see the Glossary (pg. 178).

Store leftover dressing in the refrigerator and use on green salads, potato or pasta salads or steamed greens.

Try turning this galette into a lovely hors-d'oeuvre by making them into individual tartlets.

This recipe provides a range of nutrients including vitamin B12, zinc, calcium and protein.

Varoma GF NF EF

ARTICHOKE AND BEAN RAGOUT

ACTIVE TIME 10 min | **TOTAL TIME** 1 hr 30 min | **RECIPE MAKES** 4 portions

INGREDIENTS

550 g water, plus extra for soaking artichokes

2 lemons, juice only

4 globe artichokes (see Tips)

300 g frozen broad beans, defrosted

200 g frozen green peas, defrosted

200 g sugar snap peas, cut into halves

4 garlic cloves

270 g turnips, peeled and cut into pieces (1–2 cm)

270 g potatoes, peeled and cut into pieces (1–2 cm)

4 pickling onions, cut into halves

60 g unsalted butter, cut into pieces

2 tsp Vegetable stock paste (see Tips)

100 g white wine

1 tsp dried tarragon

400 g canned black beans, rinsed and drained (approx. 250 g after draining) (optional)

5 sprigs fresh flat-leaf parsley, leaves only, torn into pieces

freshly ground black pepper, to season

USEFUL ITEMS

bowl

vegetable peeler

thermal serving bowl (ThermoServer) or other large bowl

PREPARATION

1. Fill a bowl halfway with water. Add juice from lemons.

2. Remove outer petals from artichokes and discard. Slice off top 1–2 cm of artichokes and discard. Cut artichoke stems (approx. 2 cm from base) and discard.

3. Using a vegetable peeler, peel base and stem of artichokes until light green. Cut artichokes into halves and remove furry portion (choke), leaving artichoke heart. Cut heart into halves and immediately place into bowl of lemon water (to prevent discolouration).

4. Place 500 g of the water into mixing bowl. Insert simmering basket, then weigh broad beans into it. Place Varoma dish into position and weigh green peas and sugar snap peas into it. Secure Varoma lid and steam **10 min**/**Varoma**/**speed 2**.

5. Remove simmering basket with aid of spatula. Transfer broad beans into Varoma dish with peas, and place Varoma under cold running water to cease cooking. Set aside to drain and allow broad beans to cool. Once cool enough to handle, peel broad beans and discard pods. Set beans and peas aside in Varoma. Rinse and dry mixing bowl.

6. Place garlic into mixing bowl and chop **3 sec**/**speed 7**. Scrape down sides of mixing bowl with spatula.

7. Add turnips, potatoes, onions, artichoke hearts and 30 g of the butter, then cook **5 min**/**Varoma**/↺/**speed ⌿**, **without measuring cup**.

8. Add stock paste, wine, tarragon and remaining 50 g water, then cook **7–10 min**/**100°C**/↺/**speed ⌿**, **without measuring cup**, or until all vegetables are cooked. Transfer into a thermal serving bowl (ThermoServer) or other large bowl and cover to keep warm.

9. Add black beans (optional), parsley, reserved beans and peas and remaining 30 g butter and stir to combine. Set aside for 5 minutes, then transfer into serving bowls and season with pepper. Serve immediately.

TIPS

If artichokes are not in season, use 340 g marinated artichokes (drained) and stir through in step 9.

When in season, use fresh peas and broad beans in this recipe.

Please refer to *The Basic Cookbook* or *Everyday Cookbook* for the Vegetable stock paste recipe.

The beans and peas in this recipe are good sources of both protein and iron.

To aid with digestion and reduce flatulence caused by the fibre in the beans, you may want to add a small amount (just a pinch or two) of asafoetida (see Glossary, pg. 178) during step 7. You can buy asafoetida at Indian food stores, some Asian food stores, health food stores and online.

(NF)

PUMPKIN AND TEMPEH BOBOTIE

ACTIVE TIME 20 min | **TOTAL TIME** 1 hr 5 min | **RECIPE MAKES** 6 portions

INGREDIENTS

30 g white bread (approx. 1 slice), crusts removed and torn into pieces

320 g buttermilk

1 garlic clove

1 cm piece fresh ginger, peeled

50 g brown onion, cut into quarters

1 tbsp olive oil

1 tsp ground coriander

½ tsp ground cumin

¼ tsp ground turmeric

½ tsp ground cinnamon

3 tsp curry powder

200 g tempeh, cut into pieces (2–3 cm)

40 g dried apricots

1 red apple, peeled, cored and cut into quarters

500 g pumpkin, cut into pieces (2–3 cm)

30 g lemon juice

30 g fruit chutney

50 g sultanas

1 tsp sea salt, to taste

2 pinches ground black pepper, to taste

2 eggs

4 dried bay leaves

USEFUL ITEMS

bowl

rectangular casserole dish (25 × 16 cm)

PREPARATION

1. Preheat oven to 180°C.

2. Place a bowl onto mixing bowl lid and weigh bread and 160 g of the buttermilk into it, then stir to combine. Set aside.

3. Place garlic, ginger, onion and oil into mixing bowl and chop **3 sec/speed 7**. Scrape down sides of mixing bowl with spatula.

4. Add spices and cook **3 min/100°C/speed 1**.

5. Add tempeh, apricots and apple and chop **3 sec/speed 5**.

6. Add pumpkin, lemon juice, chutney, sultanas, salt and pepper and mix **20 sec/↩/speed 2**, with aid of spatula, then cook **3 min/100°C/↩/speed 1**.

7. Add reserved bread mixture and cook **2 min/100°C/↩/speed 1**.

8. Transfer into a rectangular casserole dish (25 × 16 cm) and smooth top with spatula.

9. Without cleaning mixing bowl, place eggs and remaining 160 g buttermilk into mixing bowl and blend **15 sec/speed 6**. Pour over bobotie into casserole dish.

10. Place bay leaves on top of egg mixture and bake for 35–40 minutes (180°C). Serve immediately.

TIPS

Serve with rice, extra fruit chutney or a green salad. To find Yellow Rice recipes (a traditional South African dish), visit the Official Thermomix Recipe Community (www.recipecommunity.com.au).

This recipe provides zinc, iron, vitamin C (to aid iron absorption) and protein.

Tempeh is high in protein and can be used as a meat substitute in a variety of dishes (see Glossary, pg. 178).

Varoma **NF** **EF** **DF**

HONEY GINGER TOFU WITH GREENS

ACTIVE TIME 25 min | **TOTAL TIME** 2 hr 25 min | **RECIPE MAKES** 4 portions

INGREDIENTS

Wakame gomasio

50 g unhulled sesame seeds

50 g black sesame seeds

2 tbsp wakame flakes (see Tips)

1 tsp Celtic sea salt (see Tips)

Honey ginger tofu

700–750 g firm tofu, cut into thick slices (1.5 cm)

5 cm piece fresh ginger, peeled

2 garlic cloves

30 g rice vinegar

50 g tamari sauce

50 g honey

40 g mirin

1–2 tsp Sriracha® sauce, to taste (see Tips)

2 tsp sesame oil, plus extra for frying

Greens

500 g water

1 bunch broccolini (approx. 200 g), trimmed and cut into pieces (10 cm)

1 bunch bok choy (approx. 300 g), cut into pieces (10 cm)

50 g red onion, cut into slices (5 mm)

100 g sugar snap peas, cut into halves

1 fresh red chilli, cut into thin slices (optional)

fried shallots, for garnishing

sesame seeds, for garnishing

USEFUL ITEMS

sealable storage jar or container

casserole dish

plastic wrap

frying pan

thermal serving bowl (ThermoServer) or other large bowl

baking paper

serving plates

PREPARATION

Wakame gomasio

1. Place all wakame gomasio ingredients into mixing bowl and toast **5 min**/**Varoma**/**speed 1**.

2. Allow to cool slightly in mixing bowl (approx. 10 minutes), then mill **Turbo**/**0.5 sec**/**2 times**, or until a coarse powder. Transfer into a sealable storage container. Allow to cool completely, then seal and store until ready to use. Clean and dry mixing bowl.

Honey ginger tofu

3. Place tofu into a square or rectangular casserole dish (see Tips) and set aside.

4. Place ginger and garlic into mixing bowl and chop **3 sec**/**speed 7**. Scrape down sides of mixing bowl with spatula.

5. Add remaining tofu ingredients and warm **3 min**/**50°C**/**speed 3**. Transfer marinade into dish with tofu and ensure tofu is coated in marinade. Cover with plastic wrap and place into refrigerator to marinate for a minimum of 2 hours or overnight.

6. Place a frying pan over medium heat and add a little of the extra sesame oil. Drain tofu, reserving marinade, and add to frying pan. Cook for 1–2 minutes on each side, until warmed through and golden brown. Transfer into a thermal serving bowl (ThermoServer) or other large bowl and cover to keep warm.

Greens

7. Place water into mixing bowl. Place Varoma into position and line Varoma dish with a piece of wet, well-wrung baking paper. Place broccolini stems and bok choy stems into Varoma dish. Weigh red onion into Varoma dish, secure Varoma lid and cook **7 min**/**Varoma**/**speed 1**.

8. Add broccolini florets, bok choy leaves and sugar snap peas to Varoma dish. Drizzle vegetables with 3–4 tablespoons of the reserved marinade and sprinkle with 1–2 teaspoons of the wakame gomasio. Secure Varoma lid and steam **5–7 min**/**Varoma**/**speed 1**, or until vegetables are cooked to your liking.

9. Divide vegetables and tofu between serving plates. Garnish with sliced chilli (optional), fried shallots, sesame seeds and wakame gomasio to taste. Serve immediately.

Continued on page 138

Continued from page 136

TIPS

Unhulled sesame seeds contain more calcium and nutrients than hulled seeds, but may have a slightly bitter taste. You can use either hulled or unhulled sesame seeds in this recipe.

You can buy wakame (a type of seaweed) in health food stores or Asian food stores. For it's nutritional benefits, see the Glossary (pg. 178).

You can buy Celtic sea salt in health food stores and some gourmet food stores (see Glossary, pg. 178). You could also use standard sea salt in this recipe.

Sriracha® is a type of hot sauce often used in Thai food. You can find Sriracha® in the Asian food aisle of some supermarkets and in Asian food stores.

Wakame gomasio is a Japanese condiment and a healthier alternative to salt (see Glossary, pg. 178). Store wakame gomasio in a sealable container in a cool, dark place. Use it to season steamed rice and vegetables, as a dukkah or to flavour popcorn.

We recommend marinating tofu in a rectangular or square baking dish so that the tofu can lay flat and better absorb the marinade.

For a heartier meal, serve with steamed rice or udon noodles.

This recipe contains a number of nutrients, including calcium, zinc, vitamin C, and is a good source of protein.

NF

ZUCCHINI TORTILLAS WITH FALAFEL

ACTIVE TIME 1 hr | **TOTAL TIME** 1 day 1 hr 30 min | **RECIPE MAKES** 4 portions

INGREDIENTS

Falafels

160 g dried chickpeas

300 g water, for soaking

2 tsp coriander seeds

2 tsp cumin seeds

5 garlic cloves

1 brown onion (approx. 150 g), cut into quarters

6 sprigs fresh flat-leaf parsley, leaves only

6 sprigs fresh coriander, stalks and leaves only

4 sprigs fresh mint, leaves only

1 tsp ground black pepper

1 tsp sea salt

1 tsp paprika

1 tsp baking powder

Eggless mayonnaise

225 g grapeseed oil

85 g full cream milk

½ tsp sea salt

2 tsp lemon juice

Zucchini tortilla

oil, for greasing

120 g carrots, cut into pieces (3-4 cm)

650 g zucchini, cut into pieces (3-4 cm)

1 egg

2 tbsp plain flour

2 tsp taco seasoning (see Tips)

1–2 pinches sea salt, to taste

1–2 pinches ground black pepper, to taste

Assembly

oil, for frying

100 g rocket

½ raw beetroot, peeled and cut into matchsticks

PREPARATION

Falafels

1. Place a bowl onto mixing bowl lid and weigh chickpeas and water into it. Set aside to soak overnight.

2. Rinse and drain chickpeas and set aside. Place coriander seeds and cumin seeds into mixing bowl and roast **5 min/100°C/↻/speed ⌓**. Allow to cool (approx. 5 minutes) in mixing bowl.

3. Add garlic, onion, parsley, coriander and mint and chop **5 sec/speed 7**. Scrape down sides of mixing bowl with spatula.

4. Add drained chickpeas, pepper, salt, paprika and baking powder into mixing bowl and mix **10 sec/speed 6**.

5. Scrape down sides of mixing bowl with spatula and mix **5 sec/speed 6**, or until chickpeas are evenly chopped. Transfer mixture into a bowl, cover and place into refrigerator for 30 minutes. Clean and dry mixing bowl.

Eggless mayonnaise

6. Place a jug onto mixing bowl lid and weigh oil into it, then set aside.

7. Place milk and salt into mixing bowl and mix **20 sec/speed 7**.

8. Mix **2 min/speed 4**, slowly pouring oil onto mixing bowl lid, letting it trickle into mixing bowl.

9. Add lemon juice and mix **30 sec/speed 4**. Transfer into a sealable jar or container and place into refrigerator until ready to use. Clean and dry mixing bowl.

Zucchini tortilla

10. Preheat oven to 190°C. Lightly grease baking paper with oil and use to line 2 baking trays (30 × 40 cm) and set aside.

11. Place carrot and zucchini into mixing bowl and chop **5 sec/speed 5**. Transfer into Varoma dish and press down firmly to drain excess liquid. Set aside to drain. Rinse mixing bowl.

12. Place egg, flour, taco seasoning, salt and pepper into mixing bowl and mix **10 sec/speed 4**.

Continued on page 140

Vegetarian Kitchen

Continued from page 139

USEFUL ITEMS

bowl

jug

sealable storage jar or container

2 baking trays (30 × 40 cm)

baking paper

plate

paper towel

frying pan

4 serving plates

13. Add zucchini mixture and combine **15 sec/↻/speed 3**. Divide mixture into 4 portions and place 2 portions onto each baking tray, ensuring you leave space between each portion. Using wet hands, spread mixture into a thin circle (5 mm thickness). Bake for 30–35 minutes (190°C), or until tortilla edges are just crispy. Set aside to cool.

Assembly

14. Line a plate with paper towel and set aside. Place a frying pan over medium heat and add oil. Using wet hands, form falafel mixture into walnut-sized balls (approx. 20 balls). In batches, fry falafels for 2–3 minutes until golden brown all over. Transfer onto lined plate and allow to drain.

15. To remove tortillas from baking paper, flip tortillas over onto a plate and peel away baking paper.

16. Divide tortillas between 4 serving plates. Top tortillas with eggless mayonnaise, rocket, beetroot and falafels to serve.

TIPS

You can replace dried beans with canned beans in this recipe, however be sure to rinse and drain the canned beans prior to cooking to remove any excess sodium.

To make this recipe vegan and egg-free, replace the egg with egg substitute.

To make your own taco seasoning, place 1 tablespoon dried chilli flakes, 3 teaspoons ground cumin, ½ teaspoon garlic powder, 2 teaspoons dried onion flakes, 1 teaspoon smoked paprika, ½ teaspoon cayenne pepper, 1 teaspoon dried oregano and 2 teaspoons sea salt into mixing bowl. Roast **5–8 min/Varoma/speed 2**, or until fragrant. Allow to cool for 5 minutes in mixing bowl, then mill **30 sec/speed 10**. Transfer into a sealable jar or container until ready to use.

Mayonnaise can be made ahead of time and stored in the refrigerator. Use within 3 days of making.

Varoma GF EF

VEGETABLE CURRY WITH CAULIFLOWER COUSCOUS

ACTIVE TIME 20 min | **TOTAL TIME** 50 min | **RECIPE MAKES** 6 portions

INGREDIENTS

- 600 g cauliflower, cut into florets
- 2 tsp cumin seeds
- 3 tsp coriander seeds
- ½–1 tsp black peppercorns, to taste
- 1 tsp chilli powder
- ¼ tsp ground turmeric
- 3 garlic cloves
- 200 g brown onion, cut into halves
- 30 g vegetable oil
- 400 g coconut milk
- 130 g water
- 500 g sweet potato, cut into cubes (4 cm)
- 500 g Kent pumpkin, cut into cubes (4 cm)
- ½ tsp sea salt, plus extra to taste
- 50 g cashew nuts, plus extra, toasted, to serve
- 100 g broccolini, trimmed and cut into quarters
- 50 g snow peas, cut into halves
- 80 g fresh baby spinach leaves
- ground black pepper, to taste
- 150 g natural yoghurt
- 4 sprigs fresh coriander, leaves only, for garnishing

PREPARATION

1. Place cauliflower into mixing bowl and chop **5 sec/⟲/speed 5**. Transfer into Varoma dish and set aside. Clean and dry mixing bowl.
2. Place cumin seeds, coriander seeds and peppercorns into mixing bowl and roast **5 min/100°C/speed 1**. Allow to cool (approx. 10 minutes) in mixing bowl.
3. Add chilli powder and turmeric and mill **30 sec/speed 10**. Scrape down sides of mixing bowl with spatula.
4. Add garlic and onion and chop **3 sec/speed 5**. Scrape down sides of mixing bowl with spatula.
5. Add oil and cook **3 min/100°C/speed 1**.
6. Add coconut milk and water. Place Varoma with cauliflower into position, secure Varoma lid and cook **10 min/90°C/speed 1**. Set Varoma aside and stir cauliflower.
7. Add sweet potato, pumpkin, salt and cashews to mixing bowl. Place Varoma back into position, secure Varoma lid and cook **10–15 min/100°C/⟲/speed🥄**, or until cauliflower is cooked. Remove Varoma and set aside.
8. Add broccolini to mixing bowl and cook **2 min/100°C/⟲/speed🥄**.
9. Add snow peas and spinach, then stir to combine with aid of spatula. Cook **1 min/100°C/⟲/speed🥄**. Season with pepper to taste.
10. Serve curry with cauliflower rice and garnish with yoghurt, coriander and extra toasted cashews just before serving.

TIPS

This recipe provides vitamin C, iron, zinc and protein.

To make this recipe vegan, simply omit the yoghurt.

V EF DF

EGGPLANT WITH BURGHUL

ACTIVE TIME 10 min | **TOTAL TIME** 55 min | **RECIPE MAKES** 4 portions

INGREDIENTS

300 g burghul

1000 g water

2 garlic cloves

1 lemon, zest only, no white pith

4 spring onions/shallots, trimmed, white part cut into pieces, green part cut into thin slices

40 g soy sauce

1 tbsp mirin

1 tbsp sesame oil

2 tsp rice wine vinegar

¼ tsp ground black pepper

1 tsp raw sugar

1–2 tsp sambal oelek (see Tips)

6 sprigs fresh basil, leaves only

6 sprigs fresh mint, leaves only

40 g pumpkin seeds, roasted (see Tips)

80 g roasted pine nuts

500 g eggplant, cut into thin slices (approx. 5 mm)

olive oil, for drizzling

1–2 tsp sea salt

USEFUL ITEMS

large ceramic or glass bowl

large bowl

baking tray (30 × 40 cm)

PREPARATION

1. Place a large ceramic or glass bowl onto mixing bowl lid and weigh burghul and 500 g of the water into it. Set aside to soak for 30 minutes.

2. Transfer burghul into simmering basket, then rinse and drain. Set aside.

3. Place remaining 500 g water into mixing bowl and insert simmering basket with burghul. Place garlic on top of burghul and steam **5 min/100°C/speed 4**. Remove simmering basket with aid of spatula and set aside. Clean and dry mixing bowl.

4. Place cooked garlic, lemon zest and white part of spring onions/shallots into mixing bowl and chop **3 sec/speed 7**.

5. Scrape down sides of mixing bowl with spatula and chop **3 sec/speed 7**.

6. Add soy sauce, mirin, sesame oil, rice wine vinegar, pepper, sugar and sambal oelek and mix **5 sec/speed 5**.

7. Transfer soy sauce mixture, cooked burghul, basil, mint, pumpkin seeds, pine nuts and green part of spring onions/shallots into a large bowl and stir to combine. Set aside.

8. Preheat oven grill.

9. Place eggplant slices onto a baking tray (30 × 40 cm). Drizzle eggplant with oil and season with salt. Place under grill and grill on each side for 4–5 minutes or until slightly golden. Allow to cool slightly, then loosely roll up each slice.

10. Divide burghul mixture between 4 serving bowls. Top with rolled eggplant slices. Serve warm or cold.

TIPS

You can find roasted pumpkin seeds in most supermarkets, or you can roast your own.

The nuts and seeds in this recipe are a good source of protein.

Sambal oelek is a chilli paste often used in Indonesian and Malaysian cooking. You can find it in the Asian food section of most supermarkets and in Asian food stores.

NF EF

CHILLI CON TEMPEH

ACTIVE TIME 10 min | **TOTAL TIME** 20 min | **RECIPE MAKES** 4 portions

INGREDIENTS

1 brown onion (approx. 150 g),
cut into quarters

3 garlic cloves

1 fresh chilli, deseeded if preferred

200 g tempeh, cut into cubes (1–2 cm)

50 g extra virgin olive oil

400 g chopped canned tomatoes

1 tsp ground cumin

1 tsp ground coriander

1 cinnamon quill

1 tbsp tamari

1 tbsp mustard powder

50 g tomato paste

1–2 pinches sea salt, to taste

1 tbsp raw sugar (optional)

400 g canned kidney beans, rinsed and
drained (approx. 250 g after draining)

3 sprigs fresh coriander leaves,
to serve

100–150 g grated cheddar cheese,
to serve (optional)

200 g sour cream, to serve (see Tips)

tortillas, cut into wedges and toasted
to serve (see Tips)

lime, cut into wedges to serve

PREPARATION

1. Place onion, garlic and chilli into mixing bowl and chop **3 sec/speed 7**.

2. Add tempeh and oil and cook **4 min/100°C/↪/speed ⟲**.

3. Add tomatoes, cumin, coriander, cinnamon, tamari, mustard, tomato paste, salt and sugar (optional) and cook **8 min/100°C/↪/speed ⟲**.

4. Add kidney beans and cook **2 min/100°C/↪/speed ⟲**. Carefully remove cinnamon quill.

5. Serve with coriander, cheese (optional), sour cream, tortillas and lime wedges.

TIPS

To make this recipe vegan, omit cheese and sour cream. You can also substitute sour cream with *Cashew sour cream* (see pg. 58).

Replace tortillas with rice, freekah or corn chips.

Tempeh (see Glossary, pg. 178) is high in protein and the beans provide fibre.

You can replace canned beans with dried beans (soaked and cooked) in this recipe (see pg. 179).

To aid with digestion and reduce flatulence caused by the fibre in the beans, you may want to add a small amount (just a pinch or two) of asafoetida (see Glossary, pg. 178) during step 2. You can buy asafoetida at Indian food stores, some Asian food stores, health food stores and online.

DESSERT

NF

WHITE CHOCOLATE AND COCONUT RICE PUDDING

ACTIVE TIME 5 min | **TOTAL TIME** 35 min | **RECIPE MAKES** 6 portions

INGREDIENTS

150 g white chocolate, broken into pieces

60 g caster sugar

200 g arborio rice

400 g coconut milk

380–400 g full cream milk

2 eggs

125 g blackberries, for garnishing

USEFUL ITEMS

bowl

thermal serving bowl (ThermoServer) or other large bowl

PREPARATION

1. Place white chocolate and sugar into mixing bowl and mill **10 sec/speed 9**. Transfer into a bowl and set aside.

2. Place rice, coconut milk and 350 g of the milk into mixing bowl and cook **23–25 min/90°C/⟳/speed 1.5**, or until rice is tender.

3. Add eggs, reserved chocolate sugar and remaining 30–50 g of the full cream milk (depending on the desired thickness of your rice pudding) and combine **5 min/⟳/speed 3**.

4. Transfer into a thermal serving bowl (ThermoServer) or other large bowl and cover to keep warm. Allow to rest for a minimum of 5 minutes. Divide between 6 serving bowls, garnish with blackberries and serve immediately.

TIPS

For a thicker rice pudding, use 30 g milk in step 3; for a thinner rice pudding, use 50 g milk.

If fresh blackberries are not in season, use thawed frozen blackberries or other fresh berries of choice.

To make your own *Coconut milk*, see pg. 152.

V GF

COCONUT AND ALMOND JELLY WITH PINEAPPLE SYRUP

ACTIVE TIME 25 min | **TOTAL TIME** 1 day 1 hr 20 min | **RECIPE MAKES** 8 portions

INGREDIENTS

Almond milk

220 g whole raw almonds

660 g water

4 pitted dates

½ tsp natural vanilla extract

Coconut milk

300 g desiccated coconut

1000 g water

Jelly

200 g water, room temperature

2 tsp agar agar powder

150 g pure maple syrup

⅛ tsp natural almond extract, to taste

Pineapple Syrup

150 g fresh pineapple, flesh only, cut into pieces (1 cm)

1 tbsp orange liqueur (e.g. Grand Marnier®) (optional)

140 g water

2 tbsp soft dark brown sugar

Assembly

100 g fresh pineapple, flesh only, cut into small cubes (5 mm)

30 g coconut flakes, toasted

6 sprigs fresh mint, leaves only, cut into very thin slices

USEFUL ITEMS

ceramic or glass bowl

nut milk bag or muslin cloth

glass bowl or large jug

plastic wrap

loaf tin (25 × 10 × 7 cm)

fine mesh sieve

jug

small bowl

serving plates

PREPARATION

Almond milk

1. Place a large ceramic or glass bowl onto mixing bowl lid, then weigh almonds and water into it. Set aside to soak for 1 hour.

2. Place all ingredients, including almonds and soaking water, into mixing bowl and blend **2 min/speed 9**, until thick and creamy.

3. Pour mixture into nut milk bag or muslin cloth and firmly squeeze to extract milk into a large jug or glass bowl. Set milk aside (keep at room temperature) and discard or reserve pulp (see Tips). Clean and dry mixing bowl.

Coconut milk

4. Place coconut into mixing bowl and mill **20 sec/speed 9**.

5. Add water and blend **1 min/speed 9**. Pour mixture into a nut milk bag or muslin cloth and firmly squeeze to extract milk into a large jug or bowl. Set milk aside (keep at room temperature) and discard or reserve pulp (see Tips). Clean and dry mixing bowl.

Jelly

6. Place water, agar agar powder, syrup, almond extract and 400 g of the reserved almond milk and 400 g of the reserved coconut milk into mixing bowl and cook **8 min/90°C/speed 4**. Place any remaining almond and coconut milk into refrigerator for future use.

7. Pour jelly mixture into a loaf tin (25 × 10 × 7 cm) and allow to cool (approx. 10 minutes). Cover with plastic wrap and place into refrigerator to set overnight. Clean and dry mixing bowl.

Pineapple Syrup

8. Place all syrup ingredients into mixing bowl and chop **3 sec/speed 7**.

9. Scrape down sides of mixing bowl with spatula and cook **10–15 min/Varoma/speed 1, without measuring cup**, until syrup is thick.

10. Using a fine-mesh sieve, strain syrup into a jug and allow to cool. Set aside until ready to serve. Clean and dry mixing bowl.

Continued on page 154

Continued from page 152

Assembly

11. Place a small bowl onto mixing bowl lid, then weigh pineapple and coconut into it. Add mint leaves and stir to combine.

12. Invert loaf tin onto a work surface and carefully unmould (gently tap sides of loaf tin if required). Cut jelly into 8 thick slices, and carefully transfer onto serving plates, then drizzle with syrup and garnish with pineapple mixture to serve.

TIPS

You can find agar agar powder (see Glossary, pg. 178) at health food stores or online.

Use the leftover almond and coconut pulp in cakes, smoothies or as a base for protein balls.

You can store almond and coconut milks in the refrigerator for up to 2 days.

GF EF NF DF

BANANA TOFU ICE CREAM

ACTIVE TIME 5 min | **TOTAL TIME** 10 min | **RECIPE MAKES** 6 portions

INGREDIENTS

300 g silken tofu

4 bananas (approx. 340 g total), cut into pieces and frozen

50 g honey

250 g ice cubes

PREPARATION

1. Place all ingredients into mixing bowl and blend **1–2 min**/**speed 9**, with aid of spatula, until smooth. Serve immediately.

TIPS

For added texture, garnish with toasted nuts or desiccated coconut.

Tofu is a good source of protein, iron and calcium.

CHOCOLATE FRANGELICO® GELATO

ACTIVE TIME 15 min | **TOTAL TIME** 1 day 4 hr | **RECIPE MAKES** 4 portions

INGREDIENTS

60 g thickened cream

250 g full cream milk

500 g buttermilk

½ tsp vanilla bean paste

70 g milk chocolate, broken into pieces

70 g dark chocolate, broken into pieces, plus extra for shaving (optional)

130 g caster sugar

1 egg white

1 tbsp Frangelico®

USEFUL ITEMS

freezable containers

2 ice cube trays

plastic wrap

PREPARATION

1. Place cream, milk, buttermilk, vanilla bean paste and both milk and dark chocolates into mixing bowl and warm **5 min/37°C/speed 2**, or until chocolate melts.

2. **Insert butterfly whisk**. Add sugar and egg white and cook **8 min/90°C/speed 2**.

3. Add Frangelico® and blend **10 sec/speed 4**. **Remove butterfly whisk**. Transfer mixture into shallow freezable containers, up to 4 cm high, or 2 ice cube trays and cover with plastic wrap. Allow mixture to cool completely, then place into freezer overnight.

4. Transfer frozen gelato into refrigerator for 15 minutes, then cut into pieces (4 × 4 cm). Place half of the gelato pieces into mixing bowl and crush **20 sec/speed 6**, then mix **10 sec/speed 4** with aid of spatula. Transfer into a freezable container.

5. Place remaining gelato pieces into mixing bowl and crush **20 sec/speed 6**, then mix **10 sec/speed 4** with aid of spatula. Transfer into freezable container. Return to freezer for another 3–4 hours or until firm. Sprinkle with shaved chocolate (optional) before serving.

TIP

You can use any creamy liqueur you have available in this recipe. Omit the alcohol to make this a kid-friendly treat.

V GF R

ALMOND AND DATE BARS

ACTIVE TIME 15 min | **TOTAL TIME** 2 hr 15 min | **RECIPE MAKES** 24 portions

INGREDIENTS

80 g coconut oil, plus extra for greasing

130 g almonds

70 g cashews

250 g pitted dates

60 g desiccated coconut

20 g cocoa powder, plus extra for dusting

¼ tsp sea salt

20 g pure maple syrup

1 tbsp slivered almonds, for garnishing (optional)

1 tbsp goji berries, for garnishing (optional)

USEFUL ITEMS

rectangular baking tin (26 × 16 cm)

baking paper

small bowl

PREPARATION

1. Grease and line a rectangular baking tin (26 × 16 cm) with baking paper and set aside.

2. Place almonds and cashews into mixing bowl and chop **8 sec**/**speed 7**. Transfer into a small bowl and set aside.

3. Place dates, coconut, cocoa powder, salt and syrup into mixing bowl and chop **30 sec**/**speed 7**. Scrape down sides of mixing bowl with spatula.

4. Add reserved nut mixture and coconut oil and mix **20 sec**/**speed 5**.

5. Transfer mixture into prepared tin and press down evenly. Using a knife, score surface into 24 squares. Decorate each square with slivered almonds (optional) and goji berries (optional). Place into refrigerator until firm (approx. 2 hours).

6. Remove from tin and cut into squares. Dust with extra cocoa powder before serving or transfer into a sealable container and place into refrigerator until ready to serve.

TIP

This dish provides a good source of calcium.

(EF)

SCHIACCIATA (DESSERT PIZZA)

ACTIVE TIME 25 min | **TOTAL TIME** 2 hr 5 min | **RECIPE MAKES** 8 portions

INGREDIENTS

Pizza dough

30 g extra virgin olive oil, plus extra for greasing

220 g lukewarm water

1 tsp caster sugar

2 tsp dried instant yeast

400 g baker's flour, plus extra for dusting

1 tsp sea salt

Honey ricotta

40 g cashew nuts

250 g ricotta cheese, drained (see Tips)

30 g honey

Schiacciata

extra virgin olive oil, for greasing

500 g red seedless grapes

60 g brown sugar

USEFUL ITEMS

large bowl

plastic wrap or kitchen towel

small bowl

pizza tray

bowl

silicone bread mat (ThermoMat)

rolling pin

PREPARATION

Pizza dough

1. Lightly grease a large bowl and set aside.

2. Place water, sugar and yeast into mixing bowl and mix **20 sec**/**speed 2**.

3. Add flour, oil and salt and knead **2 min**/. Transfer dough into prepared bowl and shape into a ball. Cover bowl with plastic wrap or kitchen towel and leave to prove in a warm place until doubled in size (approx. 1 hour). Thoroughly clean and dry mixing bowl.

Honey ricotta

4. Place nuts into mixing bowl and chop **5 sec**/**speed 5**. Scrape down sides of mixing bowl with spatula.

5. Add ricotta and honey and mix **20 sec**/**speed 5**.

6. Transfer honey ricotta into a small bowl and place into refrigerator until ready to serve.

Schiacciata

7. Preheat oven to 200°C. Lightly grease a pizza tray or similar round flat tray and set aside.

8. Thoroughly wash grapes and transfer into a bowl. Add half of the sugar and gently toss to combine.

9. Transfer dough onto a lightly floured silicone bread mat (ThermoMat) or work surface. Divide pizza dough into two portions and roll out each portion into a circle (approx. 30 cm). Place one pizza base onto prepared tray.

10. Scatter half of the grapes over pizza base on tray. Place second pizza base over grapes, pushing down around the edge to seal.

11. Arrange remaining grapes on top of second pizza base and sprinkle with remaining sugar.

12. Bake for 35–40 minutes (200°C), or until golden. Serve warm with honey ricotta.

TIPS

You can replace dried yeast with 20 g fresh yeast.

If grapes are not in season, use fresh berries of choice.

To make your own ricotta, visit the Thermomix Recipe Platform (www.my-thermomix.com.au) and register to receive your free Welcome Collection, which includes a recipe for homemade ricotta.

NF

MILK TART

ACTIVE TIME 20 min | **TOTAL TIME** 3 hr | **RECIPE MAKES** 8 portions

INGREDIENTS

Base

120 g unsalted butter, chilled and cut into pieces (3–4 cm), plus extra for greasing

1 egg

100 g caster sugar

180 g self-raising flour

Filling

1 cinnamon quill

800 g full cream milk

4 eggs

40 g plain flour

40 g cornflour

200 g white sugar

1 tbsp natural vanilla extract

30 g unsalted butter

2½ tsp cinnamon sugar (see Tips)

USEFUL ITEMS

rectangular fluted tart tin (34 × 13 cm)

pie weights, rice or dried beans

baking paper

baking tray

PREPARATION

Base

1. Preheat oven to 180°C. Grease a rectangular fluted tart tin (34 × 13 cm) and set aside.

2. Place all base ingredients into mixing bowl and blend **10 sec/speed 7**, until mixture resembles breadcrumbs.

3. Transfer mixture into prepared dish and press into base and sides. Prick base with a fork or pastry docker, then line pastry base with baking paper and fill with pie weights, rice or dried beans (this will prevent pastry from rising during baking). Place tart tin onto a baking tray and bake for 15 minutes (180°C). Remove baking paper and pie weights, rice or dried beans. Bake for a further 5–7 minutes (180°C), or until base is golden. Set aside to cool. Clean and dry mixing bowl.

Filling

4. Place cinnamon quill and 400 g of the milk into mixing bowl and heat **10 min/90°C/↺/speed 1**. Set aside to infuse for 10 minutes, then remove and discard quill.

5. Add eggs, flours and sugar and blend **7 sec/speed 7**.

6. Add vanilla, butter and remaining 400 g milk and cook **16 min/90°C/speed 4**, until thick and glossy.

7. Transfer mixture into cooled tart base. Sprinkle cinnamon sugar over tart.

8. Cool slightly, then place into refrigerator for a minimum of 2 hours to set before slicing and serving.

TIP

To make your own cinnamon sugar, combine 2 tsp white sugar and ½ tsp ground cinnamon in a small bowl.

V GF R

RAW STRAWBERRY CHEESECAKE

ACTIVE TIME 15 min | TOTAL TIME 7 hr 45 min | RECIPE MAKES 12 portions

INGREDIENTS

Base

130 g macadamia nuts

140 g pitted Medjool dates

70 g desiccated coconut

¼ tsp salt

Filling

400 g raw cashew nuts, soaked
(1 hour) and drained

100 g lemons, flesh only

50 g pure maple syrup

120 g coconut oil

1 tsp natural vanilla extract

1 pinch sea salt

1 tsp balsamic vinegar

120 g water

250 g fresh strawberries

40 g fresh blueberries, for garnishing

1 tbsp goji berries, for garnishing

1 tbsp flaked almonds, for garnishing
(optional)

1 tbsp shredded coconut,
for garnishing

USEFUL ITEMS

springform cake tin (22 cm)

PREPARATION

Base

1. Place all base ingredients into mixing bowl and blend **20 sec/speed 9** until well combined and forms a moist dough. Press mixture into springform cake tin (22 cm) and place into freezer while you make filling. Clean and dry mixing bowl.

Filling

2. Place cashews, lemon flesh, syrup, coconut oil, vanilla, salt, vinegar, water and strawberries into mixing bowl and blend **1 min/speed 9**, or until smooth and creamy.

3. Pour filling over base and decorate with berries, almonds (optional) and shredded coconut. Place into freezer to set for a minimum of 6 hours or overnight.

4. Place cake into refrigerator to soften for 30 minutes, then remove from tin and transfer onto a serving platter to serve.

TIP

This dish is a good source of fibre and iron, as well as providing other nutrients and minerals such as magnesium.

V **GF** **NF**

FRUIT JELLIES

ACTIVE TIME 10 min | **TOTAL TIME** 4 hr | **RECIPE MAKES** 4 portions

INGREDIENTS

50 g fresh blueberries

50 g fresh strawberries, cut into pieces

400 g apple juice, room temperature

100 g water, room temperature

½ tsp agar agar powder

USEFUL ITEMS

4 serving bowls or glasses

PREPARATION

1. Divide blueberries and strawberries between 4 serving bowls, glasses or jelly moulds and set aside.

2. Place fruit juice, water and agar agar powder into mixing bowl and cook **6 min/90°C/speed 2**.

3. Slowly pour agar agar mixture over prepared fruit. Place into refrigerator to set for a minimum of 4 hours or overnight. Serve jellies in bowls or glasses, or turn out from moulds onto serving plates.

TIPS

You can use any type of fruit and fruit juice of choice in this recipe, however the agar agar will not set when combined with acidic fruit or fruit juice (e.g. pineapple, orange, grapefruit).

You can find agar agar powder (see Glossary, pg. 178) at health food stores or online.

POLISH CRÊPES

ACTIVE TIME 35 min | **TOTAL TIME** 3 hr 35 min | **RECIPE MAKES** 12 portions

INGREDIENTS

Quark

1000 g sour cream
(minimum 19% fat content)

Crêpe batter

330 g water

230 g full cream milk

2 eggs

20 g grapeseed oil

310 g plain flour

1 pinch sea salt

Berry sauce

200 g frozen raspberries

100 g caster sugar

20 g lemon juice (approx. ½ lemon)

Quark filling

1 egg

80 g caster sugar

1 tsp vanilla sugar (see Tips)

Assembly

unsalted butter, for frying

vanilla ice cream, to serve (optional)
(see Tips)

icing sugar, for dusting

USEFUL ITEMS

nut milk bag or muslin cloth

3 bowls

sealable storage jar or container

storage jar

1 plate

frying pan (19 cm)

PREPARATION

Quark

1. Line simmering basket with a nut milk bag or muslin cloth and set over a bowl.

2. **Insert butterfly whisk**. Place sour cream into mixing bowl and heat **40 min/90°C/speed 1**. Transfer into prepared nut milk bag. Allow to drain for 1 hour, then press out remaining liquid. **Remove butterfly whisk**.

3. Transfer quark into a sealable jar or container and place into refrigerator until ready to use. Clean and dry mixing bowl and butterfly whisk.

Crêpe batter

4. Place all crêpe ingredients into mixing bowl and mix **20 sec/speed 5**.

5. Scrape down sides of mixing bowl with spatula and mix **5 sec/speed 5**. Transfer into a bowl and set aside for 20 minutes. Clean and dry mixing bowl.

Berry sauce

6. Place all ingredients into mixing bowl and cook **6 min/90°C/speed 4**.

7. Blend **10 sec/speed 8**, then transfer into a jar and allow to cool. Place into refrigerator until ready to serve. Clean and dry mixing bowl.

Quark filling

8. **Insert butterfly whisk**. Place egg, sugar and vanilla sugar into mixing bowl and cook **2 min/60°C/speed 3**. **Remove butterfly whisk**.

9. Add 400 g of the reserved quark and mix **15 sec/speed 6**.

10. Scrape down sides of mixing bowl with spatula, then mix **10 sec/speed 6**. Transfer into a bowl and set aside.

Continue on page 170

Continued from page 168

Assembly

11. Place a frying pan (19 cm) over medium heat. Place 2½–3 tablespoons batter into frying pan and swirl to cover base. Cook for 1–2 minutes, or until edges of crêpe start to lift away from pan, then flip over and cook for 1 minute, or until golden. Place crêpe onto a plate and repeat with remaining batter, to make a total of 12 crêpes. Set crêpes aside to cool completely.

12. Spread 2 tablespoons quark filling onto crêpe. Fold crêpe in half, and then in half again and transfer onto a serving plate. Repeat with remaining quark filling and crêpes. Return frying pan to medium heat and add a little butter to pan. Add folded crêpes to pan and cook for approx. 3 minutes on each side, or until golden and warmed through.

13. Dust crêpes with icing sugar and serve warm with berry sauce and ice cream (optional).

TIPS

Also known as a farmer's cheese, quark is a soft cheese popular in Northern and Eastern Europe. Quark can also be purchased in some delis and speciality food stores.

To save time, make quark and berry sauce ahead of time.

To make your own vanilla sugar and vanilla ice cream, please refer to the recipe in *The Basic Cookbook* or *Everyday Cookbook*.

You can store quark in the refrigerator for up to 3 days. Use leftover quark to spread on toast, use in cheesecakes or use in place of ricotta in savoury tarts.

Use fresh berries instead of frozen when in season.

This recipe is a source of both calcium and protein.

(V) (GF) (R)

CHOCOLATE MOUSSE

ACTIVE TIME 10 min | **TOTAL TIME** 1 hr 10 min | **RECIPE MAKES** 4 portions

INGREDIENTS

400 g avocados, flesh only

2 tsp natural vanilla extract

¼ tsp ground cardamom

1 pinch sea salt

50 g raw cacao powder

100 g pure maple syrup

1 tbsp pistachio nuts, cut into pieces, for garnishing

1 tbsp coconut flakes, for garnishing

1 tbsp dried cranberries, for garnishing

USEFUL ITEMS

4 serving glasses

bowl

PREPARATION

1. Place avocado, vanilla, cardamom, salt, cacao powder and syrup into mixing bowl and blend **1 min**/**speed 6** until smooth.

2. Divide between 4 serving glasses and place into refrigerator to set for 1 hour.

3. Place pistachios, coconut flakes and cranberries into a bowl and stir to combine. Garnish mousse with nut mixture before serving.

TIP

Instead of nuts and coconut, try garnishing mousse with fresh seasonal berries.

COCONUT COFFEE CRUNCH

EF DF

ACTIVE TIME 20 min | **TOTAL TIME** 1 day 20 min | **RECIPE MAKES** 6 portions

INGREDIENTS

800 g coconut cream (minimum 60% coconut extract – see Tips)

120 g strong brewed coffee

60 g honey

100 g pecan nuts

120 g gingernut biscuits, cut into halves

50 g shredded coconut

1–2 bananas, cut into slices

1 tbsp carob pieces, for garnishing (optional)

USEFUL ITEMS

jug

bowl

6 serving bowls or glasses

PREPARATION

1. Place cans of coconut cream into refrigerator overnight. This will encourage cream and coconut liquid to separate.

2. Place coffee and honey into mixing bowl and cook **8 min/Varoma/speed 1**, **without measuring cup**. Transfer into a jug and set aside to cool. Clean and dry mixing bowl.

3. Place pecans into mixing bowl and roast **8 min/100°C/speed 1**. Allow to cool in mixing bowl (approx. 10 minutes).

4. Add biscuits and chop **4 sec/speed 5**, or until chunky.

5. Add shredded coconut and combine **3 sec/⟳/speed 2**. Transfer into a bowl and set aside. Thoroughly clean and dry mixing bowl.

6. **Insert butterfly whisk.** Remove coconut cream from the refrigerator and carefully scoop out a firm, thick layer of coconut cream (approx. 300 g) (see Tips). Place into mixing bowl and whip **3 min/speed 3**, or until smooth and silky, taking care not to overwhip. **Remove butterfly whisk**.

7. Place 1 tablespoon whipped coconut cream into the base of 6 serving glasses. Top each glass with 2-3 tablespoons pecan mixture, then layer with 3–4 banana slices. Top each glass with 1 tablespoon whipped coconut cream. Drizzle with 2 teaspoons reserved coffee syrup and garnish with carob pieces (optional). Serve immediately.

TIPS

It's important to use coconut cream that contains a minimum of 60% coconut cream (you will need to check the label of your coconut cream). If the coconut cream is too thin, it won't whip properly.

After removing the firm coconut cream, save the leftover liquid to use in smoothies and juices.

You can replace carob pieces with cacao nibs in this recipe.

Serve any leftover pecan mixture with yoghurt and fresh fruit for breakfast.

GF **NF**

ORANGE AND PASSIONFRUIT ETON MESS

ACTIVE TIME 40 min | **TOTAL TIME** 2 hr 50 min | **RECIPE MAKES** 6 portions

INGREDIENTS

Meringue

100 g caster sugar

3 egg whites

Passionfruit curd

80 g passionfruit pulp

40 g orange juice (approx. 1 orange)

50 g caster sugar

80 g unsalted butter, softened

3 eggs

Assembly

200 g pouring (whipping) cream

2 oranges, segmented

10 sprigs fresh mint, leaves only

USEFUL ITEMS

baking tray (30 × 40 cm)

baking paper

ceramic or glass bowl

fine mesh sieve

jug

sealable storage jar or container

6 serving plates

PREPARATION

Meringue

1. Preheat oven to 100°C. Line a baking tray (30 × 40 cm) with baking paper and set aside.

2. Place a ceramic or glass bowl onto mixing bowl lid and weigh caster sugar into it. Set aside.

3. **Insert butterfly whisk.** Place egg whites into mixing bowl and beat **2 min/37°C/speed 3.5**, **without measuring cup**, or until soft peaks form.

4. Beat **3–5 min/37°C/speed 3**, gradually adding reserved caster sugar through hole in mixing bowl lid one spoonful at a time, until sugar dissolves and stiff peaks form. **Remove butterfly whisk.**

5. Transfer meringue mixture onto prepared baking tray, spreading out to a 2 cm thickness. Bake for 80 minutes (100°C). Turn off oven and leave meringue in oven to cool for 1 hour. Clean and dry mixing bowl and butterfly whisk.

Passionfruit curd

6. Strain passionfruit pulp through a fine-mesh sieve into a jug. Reserve any remaining pulp and seeds.

7. **Insert butterfly whisk.** Place passionfruit juice, orange juice, sugar, butter and eggs into mixing bowl and cook **8 min/80°C/speed 3**.

8. Check to see if mixture has reached setting point by inserting a spoon into curd. Curd should coat the back of the spoon in a thick layer. If curd is not set, cook for a further **2–3 min/80°C/speed 3**, or until thickened. **Remove butterfly whisk.**

9. Transfer curd into a sealable jar or container and set aside to cool to room temperature, then place into refrigerator until cold. Clean and dry mixing bowl and butterfly whisk.

Assembly

10. **Insert butterfly whisk.** Place cream into mixing bowl and whip **30–40 sec/speed 4**, or until soft peaks form. **Remove butterfly whisk.**

11. To assemble, dollop 2–3 teaspoons passionfruit curd and 2–3 teaspoons whipped cream onto 6 serving plates in any pattern you like. Break meringue into shards and decorate each plate with 1–2 meringue pieces. Garnish with orange segments, mint leaves and reserved passionfruit pulp and seeds. Serve immediately.

Varoma (GF) (NF) (EF)

PEACHES IN WHITE WINE SYRUP

ACTIVE TIME 10 min | **TOTAL TIME** 4 hr | **RECIPE MAKES** 4 portions

INGREDIENTS

6–8 peaches, depending on size

100 g pure maple syrup

600 g white wine

300 g water

2 cinnamon quill

1 vanilla bean, cut into halves lengthways and seeds scraped

80 g lemon juice (approx. 2 lemons)

6 pieces lemon zest (7 × 1 cm), no white pith

3 star anise

1–2 sprigs fresh mint, leaves only, to serve

Greek yoghurt, to serve (optional)

USEFUL ITEMS

sealable container

PREPARATION

1. Using a sharp knife, gently score a cross in the top and bottom of each peach. Place peaches into Varoma and set aside.

2. Place all remaining ingredients, except mint and yoghurt, into mixing bowl. Place Varoma into position, secure Varoma lid and cook **20–40 min**/**Varoma**/↻/**speed 1**, until peaches are softened and skin has started to peel away (cooking time will vary depending on the ripeness of the peaches; riper peaches will take less time to soften).

3. Set Varoma aside and allow peaches to cool completely. Once cooled, peel skin from peaches and discard. Remove pits (if desired) and place peaches into a sealable container. Pour white wine syrup over peaches and place into refrigerator for a minimum of 3 hours to cool completely. Gently turn peaches occasionally as they cool to coat them in syrup.

4. Garnish peaches with mint leaves and serve with syrup and yoghurt (optional).

TIP

Serve leftover syrup over ice cream, drizzled over berries or use it to flavour sparkling water or sparkling wine.

GLOSSARY

Agar agar powder
A gelatinous substance derived from seaweed, it is used as a thickening agent and is often a vegan substitute for gelatine. It dissolves best in hot liquids, then requires refrigeration to set.

Asafoetida powder
Asafoetida comes from the root of a perennial herb cultivated in India. It's often used in Indian cuisine, particularly in vegetable and legume dishes. It has a strong odour, but the aroma softens as it cooks, and tastes similar to onion and garlic, enhancing the savoury flavour of the dish. It helps reduce flatulence and constipation, and reduces the growth of microflora in the gut. A little goes a long way, so only a small amount (a pinch or two) is needed.

Buckwheat
Not actually wheat, but a fruit seed that resembles a grain in appearance. Buckwheat is gluten free and used as an alternative to rice or rolled oats.

Bragg's® liquid aminos
A liquid protein concentrate derived from soybeans. It's often used as an alternative to tamari and soy sauce.

Burghul
Is a common ingredient in Indian and Middle Eastern dishes. Often served in place of rice or couscous, burghul adds a light, nutty flavour to dishes.

Cacao powder
Cacao is the purest form of chocolate and is less processed than cocoa. It has high levels of antioxidants and is a great substitute for chocolate in smoothies and desserts. You can find it in the health food aisle of major supermarkets and health food stores.

Carob
Carob can be used as a substitute for cocoa and chocolate. Be sure to check the label if you are using carob as a dairy free alternative to chocolate.

Celtic sea salt
An unrefined sea salt that is naturally found in the northwest coast of France, near the Celtic sea. It is sun-dried to preserve the live enzymes, is unprocessed and contains few if any added chemicals or preservatives.

Chia seeds
These wholegrain, gluten free seeds contain a wealth of vitamins and minerals, plus calcium, iron and fibre.

Coconut oil
A non-animal saturated fat high in nutrients, especially useful for those following vegan and dairy free diets. It has a moderate smoke point, making it suitable for frying. It's also very versatile, since it is solid at room temperatures and liquid when warm. Store at room temperature.

Cold-pressed oils
For any oil to be considered cold-pressed, the heat produced through pressing of the fruit and seeds must not exceed 49°C. The benefits of cold-pressed oils include stronger flavour, aroma and increased nutritional value as nutrients are not lost from heating (such as some avocado oils).

Daikon
Also known as "Japanese horseradish", daikon has a mild flavour and can be eaten cooked, pickled or raw.

Flaxseeds (linseeds)
These small brown seeds provide nutrients, including calcium and iron. They provide a slight nutty flavour; ideal for smoothies, breads and cereal toppings.

Junket tablets
These flavourless tablets help form milk curds, cheeses and ice cream. They often contain rennet (enzymes produced by ruminant animals).

Kombu
An edible Japanese seaweed that is either sold in dried or pickled form, and is a good source of iodine. It is a great condiment to flavour savoury dishes, such as beans or soups.

Millet
A cereal grain made from grass seeds that can be milled into flour, or cooked in porridge or used as a substitute for rice. They contain fiber, iron, calcium, and B vitamins.

Miso paste
High in protein and rich in vitamins and minerals, miso is a fermented soy paste widely used in Japanese cooking. It comes in white, yellow and red. The darker the miso, the stronger the flavour.

Mirin
This sweet rice wine is used often in Japanese cooking.

Molasses
The dark liquid by-product created from refining sugar cane.

Organic puffed rice
Contains only the natural rice grain and can be found in the health food aisle of most major supermarkets.

Polenta
Polenta is made using cornmeal and is versatile enough to be used both dry and cooked. We used fine and coarse polenta, as instant polenta can cook too quickly and become gluggy.

Quinoa (red/white)
High in fibre and one of the few plant foods that is considered to be a complete protein.

Quinoa flakes
Made from steamed and rolled quinoa seeds. These are a great alternative to rolled oats.

Sambal oelek
A spicy paste used in Indonesian and Malaysian cooking.

Savoury yeast flakes
These yellow flakes of deactivated yeast are used for flavouring non-dairy dishes that require a 'cheesy' flavour, and are usually fortified with vitamin B12.

SOAKING AND COOKING BEANS

Soba noodles
Thin, buckwheat flour noodles.

Sriracha® sauce
A Thai hot sauce used as a condiment or dipping sauce.

Sumac
This spice has a lemony flavour and is often used in Middle Eastern cooking. You can find it in most major supermarkets.

Tahini
This nutty-flavoured paste is made from hulled or unhulled sesame seeds, which provide a good source of calcium.

Tamari
The salty liquid by-product of miso as it matures. Tamari is usually wheat free and similar in taste to soy sauce, although less salty.

Tempeh
Originating in Indonesia, tempeh is made by fermenting the whole soy bean, which makes it firmer than tofu and gives it a unique texture. It provides a variety of minerals and is quite high in protein. It is widely available in Asian supermarkets as well as most major supermarkets.

Tofu
Made from soy milk curds, there are many varieties of tofu (both fresh and processed). Tofu has very little flavour or smell, making it versatile enough to use in both savoury and sweet dishes. It is low in calories, high in iron and contains no saturated fats.

Wakame flakes
This edible seaweed (or sea vegetable) has a subtle sweet flavour and is most often served in soups and salads, or used to make the condiment Wakame gomasio. It provides calcium, iron, some B vitamins as well as a variety of other minerals.

Xanthan gum
Produced by bacterial fermentation of corn sugar, and used as a gel or thickener. It's often used in gluten free baking as a binding agent.

We have used both dried and canned beans (drained and rinsed) in *Vegetarian Kitchen*. You can substitute dried beans for canned beans in some recipes, ensuring you thoroughly rinse and drain the canned beans prior to cooking.

You can substitute some of the canned beans with dried beans by following the below soaking and preparation steps.

Dried beans to cooked weight

BEANS	DRIED	COOKED
Cannellini beans	100–110 g	Approx. 250 g
Kidney beans	100–110 g	Approx. 250 g
Mixed beans	100–110 g	Approx. 250 g
Chickpeas	100 g	Approx. 250 g

Soaking dried beans
Place 1:6 ratio of beans to warm water (60˚C) then:

Quick soak: Place a large pot over low-medium heat (60˚C) and boil beans for 2 minutes. Remove from heat, cover and leave to stand for 1 hour. Drain and cook.

OR

Long soak (preferred method): Place beans into a bowl of warm, filtered water and allow to soak overnight or up to 48 hours at room temperature. Drain and rinse beans 2-3 times during the soaking process. Drain and cook.

Cooking
Place 200 g (maximum) soaked beans into simmering basket and insert simmering basket into mixing bowl. Place 900 g water into mixing bowl and cook **60 min/90˚C/speed 3**. If beans are not cooked after 60 minutes, top up with water to 500 ml mark and cook a further **30 min/90˚C/speed 3**, then check again.

INDEX

FIND US ONLINE

Join the conversation! We'd love to receive your comments and photos via our website, Recipe Community and social media channels. You can also join more than just the conversation – visit our website to learn how to turn your Thermomix passion into a business.

THERMOMIX WEBSITE

Visit our website for all things Thermomix. Book a demo, register for a cooking class, learn how to start your own Thermomix business or visit our online store where you can purchase cookbooks and accessories conveniently.
thermomix.com.au
thermomix.co.nz

THERMOMIX RECIPE COMMUNITY AND FORUM

Join the Thermomix Recipe Community and access thousands of recipes from around Australia and New Zealand. The site also features a forum for users to find and share hints and tips. Register for free at **recipecommunity.com.au**

MY-THERMOMIX RECIPE PLATFORM

The new My-Thermomix Recipe Platform is a centralised online library that allows you to access exclusive recipes created for the platform, as well as recipes on your Recipe Chips. You can also create meal plans and shopping lists to streamline your shopping.
Visit **www.my-thermomix.com.au** and register today to receive your free recipe collection of our top 10 favourite recipes.

SOCIAL MEDIA

Facebook:
facebook.com/thermomixinaustralia
facebook.com/
thermomixinnewzealand
YouTube: ThermomixAustralia
Twitter: @thermomixaus

Instagram:
@thermomixaus @thermominz
#thermomixaus and #thermomixnz
Pinterest: pinterest.com/thermomixaus
pinterest.com/thermomixnz

NOTES